The Computer Revolution

The Computer Revolution

Benjamin B. Wells

Nova Science Publication, Inc.
Commack, NY

Assistant Vice President/Art Director: Maria Ester Hawrys
Graphics: Frank Grucci
Editorial Production: Susan Boriotti
Office Manager: Annette Hellinger
Acquisitions Editor: Tatiana Shohov
Book Production: Ladmila Kwartirof, Christine Mathosian,
Joanne Metal and Tammy Sauter
Circulation: Iyatunde Abdullah, Cathy DeGregory and Annette Hellinger

Library of Congress Cataloging-in-Publication Data

Wells, Benjamin B.
Computer revolution / by Benjamin B. Wells.
p. cm.
Includes index.
ISBN 1-56072-498-6
1. Computer and civilization. 2. Computers. I. Title.
QA76.9C66W47 1997 97-41704
371.33'4--dc21 CIP

6080 Jericho Turnpike, Suite 207
Commack, New York 11725
Tele. 516-499-3103 Fax 516-499-3146
E Mail: Novascience@earthlink.net
Web Site: http://www.nexusworld.com/nova

Printed in the United States of America

CONTENTS

PREFACE ix

REVOLUTIONARY PROMISES 1

THE VANGUARD OF THE REVOLUTION 2

THE QUEST FOR MACHINES THAT THINK, LEARN AND TEACH 9

COMPUTERS IN THE CLASSROOM 15

COMPUTER CITIZENSHIP 25

COMPUTERS IN THE CLASSROOM: EDUCATORS' APPROACHES 29

MODERN APPROACHES OF EDUCATORS 35

COMPUTERS AND INTUITION 39

THE ROMANCE OF COMPUTERS 45

NEANDERTHAL LISA 46
EMOTION AND LEARNING 49

EDUCATIONAL SOFTWARE 51

RECENT TRENDS 56

COMPUTER GAMES 61

THE ELECTRONIC CLASSROOM 65

THE NETWORKED CLASSROOM 68
THE COMPUTER ROOM 70

COMPUTERS IN THE CLASSROOM: BIG BUSINESS 71

APPLES FOR THE CLASSROOM 73
SAFEWAY CASH REGISTER TAPES FOR CLASSROOM COMPUTERS 74
PRIVATIZATION OF PUBLIC SCHOOLS 75

ACADEMICIANS' VIEWS OF COMPUTERS IN THE CLASSROOM 77

COMPUTERS IN ACADEMIA 83

CAMPUS NETWORKS 84
COMPUTERS IN LAW SCHOOL 86
ELECTRONIC SCHOLARLY JOURNALS 88

COMPUTERS FOR RESEARCH 91

COMPUTER ART 95

COMPUTER TALK 97

MARKETING TALK 100

COMPUTERS IN THE WORKPLACE 103

"REAL WORK" IS DONE ONLY AT A COMPUTER TERMINAL 103
THE PAYOFF FROM COMPUTERIZATION 106
E-MAIL AND INTRA-OFFICE COMMUNICATIONS 109
COORDINATION THEORY 109
THE DUMBING DOWN OF AMERICA 111
THE NEW WORK ORDER 112
COMPUTER GAMES IN THE WORKPLACE 114
COMPUTER RELATED INJURIES 115
COMPUTER SCIENTISTS ON COMPUTERS IN THE WORKPLACE 116

INFORMATION SUPERHIGHWAY 119

THE VISION: THE KNOWLEDGE NAVIGATOR 119
THE REALITY: THE INTERNET 120
CYBERBANKING 126
VEHICLES FOR THE HIGHWAY 130

COLD FUSION 132

VIRTUAL REALITY-VIRTUAL NONSENSE 135

THE MYTH OF INTERACTIVITY 135
VIRTUAL WORLDS 140

ARMAGEDDON: THE YEAR 2000 143

PC OR TV? 151

BATTLES WON 153

SOFTWARE: THE RIGHT STUFF 155
SUPER COMPUTERS 156
COMPUTERS OF THE FUTURE 157
PERSONAL COMPUTERS OF THE FUTURE 160
SOFTWARE OF THE FUTURE 161

CONCLUSIONS 163

REFERENCES 169

INDEX 173

PREFACE

It's about 2 o'clock in the afternoon on Thursday at the Arlington County Central Library. The library's patrons are a mix of students, retirees, and unemployed. Biweekly unemployment checks arrive on Thursdays, and one can see the torn narrow envelopes cast about in trashcans. The men are scruffy and a little seedy, but some are groomed and have put on suits as if going off to the office to partake of the day's business transactions. Some had been employed doing research under defense contracts that disappeared following the collapse of the Soviet Union. All have a vacant, unhappy look.

A special section of the library is devoted to job hunters and career builders: a bulletin board posted with job openings, volumes filled with information on hundreds of companies around the country, and how-to-interview and self-help books of every variety. Many job seekers, however, eschew this section in favor of the growing collection of computer instruction books complete with floppy disks embedded inside the back cover. Large paperback books with titles such as "Learn C++ in 21 Days," or "Teach Yourself Unix." Each weekend advertisements in the newspaper scream out for people with these and other computer skills.

Gone are the card catalogues, replaced by rows of interactive terminals to access titles, authors, and subjects in the library's modest collection. The most popular new library additions are the personal computers set up in the children's room. They run such programs as Supermunchers, a vocabulary game, and Millie's Math House. Thirty minutes of computer time can be booked, but the earliest booking is not available within a week. The parents, who call for reservations, usually can't afford a computer at home. Many are recent immigrants struggling to support a family and to make their way into mainstream America.

On the upper level of the library a booth has been set up with a prominent sign proclaiming "Internet." A middle aged lady sits alone, unoccupied at a terminal, awaiting requests from library patrons.

What is happening at Arlington Central Library is happening at libraries across the nation. "There will continue to be a large percentage of people who can't afford to own computers, and we will serve that population," said George Needham, executive director of the Public Library Association. "That's a big goal of public libraries, to try to prevent a bigger gap between information haves and information have-nots[26]."

The libraries on the Berkeley campus are excellent. No riffed or laid-off workers here, only students and faculty. Mathematics has its own separate library housed in the same building as the department itself. All of the mathematics journals come there too. During the days of turmoil the library was always a place of sanctuary just as it is now. You could go in and sit down in the quiet away from the anti-Vietnam war protests and away from the Mario Savio speeches.

The 60s were exciting times at Berkeley. Every weekday morning around 11 o'clock "Preacher Sam" would take up residence at the corner of Telegraph Avenue and Shattuck. Standing atop a wooden crate and with bible in hand, redheaded snaggle-toothed Sam would begin his sermons in his familiar Southern-Country drawl. Soon a knot of people would gather, and by noon he had a respectable congregation of curious onlookers and hagglers.

Arguments frequently broke out, and indeed Sam seemed to welcome them. Most of his antagonists professed atheism, and Sam was well aware of what he was up against. Sam was a missionary, not a missionary in a foreign land, but a missionary in his own country. Back in the small Christian community his congregation had decided that there were sinners enough right here in the USA. Why send a missionary to some exotic far-off land, when in their very own country there was a place as sinful and heathen as any in the world-Berkeley, California?

At Berkeley, we really didn't know that we were in the midst of three revolutions: one social, another political, and the third an intellectual revolution. The social one fought for desegregation and justice for minorities, mainly blacks. Campus groups such as the Student Non-violent Coordinating Committee (SNCC),(better known as "Snick"), energized and supported integration activities taking place in Alabama and other places around the country. The campus was transformed into a buzzing factory of social discourse.

The political revolution was fought on two related fronts. One front addressed the unfolding war in Vietnam and the second the rights of students to engage in political activities on campus, the much-heralded Free Speech Movement. It has been said that protesting the war in Vietnam by implication meant protesting the march of computer technology[4]. In any event, what happened at Berkeley was watched very closely by the rest of the world and set the stage for a nation to rethink its course.

The third revolution, the intellectual one, was midwife to a rebirth of the belief in science and pure reason as a means to save the world. More than that idealism, among my group the sheer enjoyment of mathematics and teaching was seen as a noble way to dedicate one's life. Our heroes were the old lions who had made their mark and attached their names to important results. Names like Tarski, von Neumann, and Robinson.

Most of us who passed the qualifying examinations and wrote a doctoral thesis followed career paths as university professors. Those who did not were awarded the "Master's consolation prize" and pursued careers at government labs, industry, and business.

Many in this latter group learned about computers, which at the time meant the big "mainframes." There was much to learn about the subject, the machines were not so "user-friendly," and even then the demand for competent "systems administrators" was significant. Universities, for example, were beginning to make use of the mainframes to keep administrative records and help with registration. There was no inkling of the deluge to come.

Many of the 60s radicals, including some of those at Berkeley, went on to embrace the computer culture. One of the most notable examples is Timothy Leary, the former Harvard professor and LSD mind-trip advocate of the 60s counter-culture. In the 1990s, with consistency second to none, Leary became an advocate for computer-based virtual reality[4].

Ever the media hound, Leary in his mid seventies and with advanced prostate cancer laid out his plans to terminate his life--on the Internet! In the sixties he preached that one could find truth in pills and cubes of LSD; in the nineties he claimed one can find the same truth within a PC. Leary passed away a few months ago, and if there were an "event" on the net, I didn't get word of it.

At the vanguard of modern technology, the computer has spawned an unbelievably broad spectrum of human endeavor as well as behavior. A few short weeks ago a reporter from the San Francisco Chronicle called to ask whether I knew Ted Kaczynski, the now infamous unibomber suspect. The question was a reasonable one, but the answer was no, although our paths might have crossed, since he arrived at the Berkeley mathematics department only a few short weeks before I departed back in 1967. I'm sure reporters have been calling anyone who might have had occasion to have had any contact whatsoever with that enigma.

It is ironic that the actions of the unibomber make it even more difficult to question the benefits of any technology. Insane and criminal acts in support of an extreme point of view tend to validate the entire spectrum of opposing views. Suffice it to say, sane people do not advocate doing away with computers and other technological advancements in favor of a stone-age existence.

The subject matter of this book emphasizes two principal branches of the computer revolution. The first branch is education and the attempt to define the computer's role in the learning process.

The second is the transformation of the workplace by computer technology.

An examination of these branches necessarily leads us into an examination of related areas. The effort to produce machines that teach has paralleled the effort to produce machines that learn. Thus the subject of computers in education is necessarily related to the subject of artificial intelligence.

There are other subjects of recent importance that impinge on both education and the workplace. The first example that comes to mind is the Internet, but there are others. The subject of computer games may not seem to be in either category, but only a brief look at this subject is enough to convince one that it has relevance both in education as well as in the workplace.

What is the computer's role in research? After all, most research is carried out in a "workplace" environment. Has the computer been as great a boon to basic research as it has undoubtedly been to applied research?

There is a problem with computer software that has become widely known as the "Year 2000 Problem" or the Millenium Bug. It serves to benchmark the extent computers have penetrated our social and economic fiber. But it is also a happy reminder of how fundamentally trivial they can be, how dependent they are on humans for their care and feeding. As the fateful date approaches, a large chunk of corporate and governmental resources will be devoted to making the problem go away.

The computer revolution is no longer in its infancy. Over thirty years have elapsed since the first mainframes came on line, and it's been over twenty since personal computers were introduced into the classroom and into the workplace. A critical evaluation of the effects and worth of these machines should therefore be possible. In view of tight educational budgets and the tremendous corporate outlays for computer systems, such an evaluation would seem desirable.

CHAPTER 1

REVOLUTIONARY PROMISES

The much-heralded personal computer (PC) leads the revolutionary procession. It leads by virtue of its prominence and visibility in schools, the workplace, and day-to-day existence. What is a PC anyway? It's a misnomer whose primary function has been usurped. It has evolved into more of a communicator or electronic notebook than a computer. How many people do you know who use their PC for computing? I know one such person, a dedicated engineer who does research at home in acoustic propagation.

One of the ironies of the computer revolution is that the modern PC, say something like a 133 megahertz Pentium which is now more or less middle-of-the-road, has tremendous computing power. For under $2,000 you can have a machine more powerful than the mainframes of just a few years ago.

The typical Mac or PC Windows user "points and clicks" the "mouse" at icons on the screen. Files of English text are opened, read, and sometimes written. And now with the Internet, you can do these things with files that reside in machines half way around the world. The big deal is that computer links can outrun a team of good librarians with fax machines.

Ten short years ago computers meant something different. They meant something that was closer to actual computing. The public mind envisioned them as "thinking machines." Back then the future of computers was to become artificial brains in the service of mankind.

THE VANGUARD OF THE REVOLUTION

In spite of the new definition and direction of the computer revolution, extravagant claims about the ability of computers to achieve artificial intelligence (AI) and to assume a central role in teaching continue to be heard. The projected time for the coming of many of these benefits has passed, and they are as yet unfulfilled. Indeed, attempts to realize cognitive AI have been largely abandoned.

Promises made back in 1967 by artificial intelligence guru Marvin Minsky that "Within a generation the problem of creating 'artificial intelligence' will be substantially solved" are now denied. This was no slip of the tongue. In 1970 he reiterated, "In three to eight years we will have a machine with the general intelligence of a human being."

In accepting the 1994 Allan Turing Award from the Association of Computing Machinery, Raj Reddy, dean of Computer Science at Carnegie Mellon University responded. "Who made these promises? As far as I know, no one has promised anything other than that we will create artifacts that exhibit intelligence..."

Is it so serious a crime to make rhetorical promises to the community at large and then not to keep them? No court of law could award "damages." And yet there have been damages. Based on those promises, a great deal of money has been spent, and little has resulted from the investment. By the year 1987, equity investment by corporate America in AI topped the $100 million mark[47], most of the spending occurring in only the four-year period 1983-1987. This does not count the many millions that went to AI from government agencies such as the Defense Advanced Research Projects Agency (DARPA), as well as venture capital outlays. Although these numbers do not seem extravagant when compared to other types of corporate and governmental investments, they represented a considerable percentage of funds available for basic research. At a time when AI was lavishly funded, worthwhile and legitimate scientific causes were going hungry.

Educators predicted in parallel with their AI colleagues that the computer would assume a central role in teaching. This was to occur within the span of less than two decades. It has been three decades, much money has been spent, and student performance has declined significantly over the period.

Nevertheless, the claims are repeated ever more stridently. Perhaps because of this, there is a growing realization that everything is not working out for the best, that somehow the revolution has been over-sold. There is a sense that many of the areas that computers have opened up are fragile or ephemeral. Even worse, some elements of the revolution have the trappings of a cult.

For over thirty years the gurus of one cult have touted the computer as a miracle machine able to teach children. In April 1995 the results of a national study were announced that showed over a third of school age children, first grade through high-school, are reading significantly below grade level. These results show a significant decline in the reading abilities of the nation's children. Is it possible that these results would have been even poorer without the intervention of computers in the classroom?

"Wait a minute!" say the gurus. "The educational software that we've been using is not the right kind. We think we know the right kind, and it's being developed as we speak. We know because we can give impressive demonstrations of the success that computer and calculator classroom use has enjoyed with groups we've worked closely with in Los Angeles and in other large cities."

The computer revolution is multi-faceted. Its social component is as great as its technical one. When all of its branches are examined, one must conclude that it is often more about form than it is about substance. The common belief now is that a computer by itself has very limited utility. It must be "networked" to enable it to "talk" to tens or hundreds of other computers across the hall and across the continent. It must become an instrument of the "Information Superhighway." A computer by itself is likened to a modern automobile in the middle of the jungle, a thing of wonder perhaps, but useless without a highway system to drive upon.

The information superhighway has inspired a cult-like following. In the 1980s the Internet computer network grew up to link universities, government entities, and scientists all over the globe. This was good; science requires communication to be productive. But now the Internet is inundated with people having diverse and decidedly nonscientific purposes. Most of them are wasting time, including some scientists whose time would be more productively spent in teaching or research.

The backbone of the information highway, the Internet, doesn't yet work quite right: searching for information is time consuming and haphazard, graphics are often slow and difficult, and your message might get lost or go to the wrong person. Even worse, you might not even be aware of it. None of this has prevented the millions (some say 20 million) from getting on the "net" and firing e-mail back and forth to one another in a flurry of communication that is reminiscent of what happened in citizen-band radio of the sixties and seventies.

"Never mind," say the gurus. "The glitches will be fixed, and the information superhighway will transform the way we think and do business. Indeed, it already has. We are becoming the 'information society.' Wealth will be measured in terms of the amount of information you command."

If that's the case, then I wonder why I'm not richer; I thought that I knew a lot, or at least I used to. Ah, ha! say the gurus, that's not the kind of information we mean. We are speaking of the kind of information that goes into data bases; information such as, "the number of cubic feet of natural gas that was consumed between October 1993 and March 1994 in Frederick County, Maryland."

When the wheel was invented, there must have been legions of naysayers who predicted the demise of man's physical strength and stamina that would come about as a result of his reliance on a passive conveyance. There must have been a million good reasons why the device could not succeed. Certainly that was the case with the invention of the automobile: Man was not meant to travel at the ungodly speed of twenty miles per hour. If there is a bit of naysaying of computer technology in some quarters, it is drowned out many times over by its outspoken advocates.

The computer can be a valuable tool, but it is only a tool, and it is when we try to misuse a tool do we encounter negative consequences. Too much is expected of these machines because of the piled-on layers of jargon and hype. Often they don't do anything more that couldn't have been done just as quickly, cheaply, and more reliably by picking up the telephone, sending a fax, mailing a letter, or using common sense.

A very large percentage of personal computers is dedicated to word processing. Indeed, this task has been the engine that has driven the explosion of the PC culture. With evermore "user-friendly" software, crafting a letter-perfect document has become easier and faster. Yet, even so, I sometimes wonder about the truthfulness of that statement.

When I was a boy in the early 1950s my father was hard at work writing voluminous chapters of medical textbooks. After doing his initial research, he would speak the words of his writings into a recording machine called a Dictaphone. I remember it quite well. He held a microphone attached to a machine that wrote onto a thin flexible plastic disk. He could play back his words just spoken, go back and write over errors, advance the recording head to a new position on the disk, etc. The next day, or whenever the work was done, he presented the disk to a typist who would play back his words and render the typewritten copy.

If he were alive today, my father would, no doubt as do most authors, have a word processor on his desk but no secretary to transcribe his work. Would his workload have been significantly reduced? As advanced as the capabilities of the multi-media PCs have become, none as yet has the capability of accomplishing all the steps just described. In particular, difficulties are still encountered with translating the spoken word to finished text.

One good reason to view the revolution with suspicion is the fountain of "technoneologisms" that spew forth. Technobabble attempts to hide a content void or to conceal a lack of novelty.

For example, consider that ubiquitous oxymoron *virtual reality.* All computer functions have the effect of blurring reality. When we point and click at the icons on the terminal, even a child recognizes that they are stand-ins for something that has, or at least could have, a physical realization. Virtual reality is at the heart of the computer revolution because it represents the ultimate in the blurring of reality.

As an applied technology, virtual reality has been at work for years (although it wasn't called that) in the form of aircraft simulation modules for pilot training. The reality that they simulate so approximates the real thing that these useful machines can train airline pilots without risking lives and equipment.

Although it's difficult to find substance in most recent virtual reality, some interesting applications have been found, however, in the area of cognitive therapy. For example, a virtual reality trek across a high bridge has been used with some success to overcome the fear of heights.

Just as pilots have been trained in flight simulators, physicians may now practice "virtual surgery" for certain operations before attempting the real thing on flesh and blood patients. In fact, any procedure requiring physical dexterity could conceivably be practiced first via a virtual reality set-up. First you would want to be sure, however, that the savings would justify the cost of development of the virtual reality equipment and software.

A close cousin of virtual reality is the highly successful and useful set of tools developed for architectural, engineering, and mechanical design, namely computer aided design (CAD) and computer aided manufacturing (CAM) software. CAD/CAM has been around for more than twenty years but doesn't have a fraction of the tabloid glitz of virtual reality.

To be sure, computers have proved to be reliable and useful servants in a multitude of tasks, many unseen and taken for granted: navigation computers for aircraft; dynamic data base systems to manage large inventories for hospitals, schools, and government; reservation booking systems for hotels, airlines, and trains. Curiously, these tasks are ones for which the term *computer* is appropriate to its original meaning. The list is well known and now extends to almost every business enterprise.

Who could deny the greater convenience and enhanced searching power of computerized card catalogs in the library when compared to the old bulky paper ones? Except when the computer "goes down" is there ever any doubt about its ability to perform these tasks more efficiently and at lower cost than the older human-based systems.

This book highlights two widespread uses of computers that are misguided and are having damaging consequences: namely computers as currently used in the classroom as a teaching tool and computers as they are often misused in the workplace to create the illusion of useful work. In both cases the ill effects of the misguided use of computers are insidious. They are insidious because the illusion is created that learning has taken place in the first case and that work has been done in the second case.

Some authors have attacked the invasion of computers into the workplace and classrooms as somehow dehumanizing. They say that it's better to smell one real flower than to see all of the gardens of the world on a video monitor. While that may be true, I believe that such arguments are not solidly grounded. Are rocket ships or cars dehumanizing? In a sense they certainly are, but to rail against them is to fail to understand what humanity is about. We shall try to avoid having our arguments in this book depend upon any charge of dehumanization or even social alienation by computers.

Although it might be exciting to do so, we will not dwell on the occasional devastating impact of the failure of computers in, for example, recent airplane and train crashes. Certainly the kind of computer failures that recently blinded California air traffic controllers are frightening enough. But in spite of such failures, no one could argue that computers have not made air travel quicker and safer.

Nor are we interested in the areas of computer snooping and computer crime. It's entertaining to read about the hackers who recently broke into Citibank's computers somewhere in the former Soviet Union and stole millions. These and similar areas are well covered in a recent book by Peter Newmann.[46]

There are other facets of computers that we shall only mention in passing, for example, computer fatigue and the stress that can result from using or not being able to use computers. These are subjects that have been discussed and written about for many years. Indeed the whole field of ergonomics was invented to address ailments related to physical fatigue resulting from the extended use of keyboard and screen.

CHAPTER 2

THE QUEST FOR MACHINES THAT THINK, LEARN, AND TEACH

It would be surprising if all of the expectations engendered by the computer revolution, or indeed by any revolution, were vindicated. Many of these expectations have been generously fulfilled. Some, however, are still awaiting fulfillment. Almost half a century ago mathematician and computer pioneer Alan Turing prophesied that machines could be made to exhibit human-like intelligent behavior. After many years and even more attempts, the goal of producing such machines is no closer to realization.

Research in cognitive artificial intelligence (AI), what Hubert Dreyfus[22] calls "Good Old Fashioned AI," is for all intents and purposes dead. The very name itself has fallen into disfavor. Only a handful of the dozens of AI companies, begun with such fanfare and promise in the 1980s, remain. And even they are developing and marketing object-oriented software and other commercial products unrelated to cognitive AI.

That is not to say that enthusiasm is diminished in all quarters, nor that impressive demonstrations have not been made in limited domains. It does mean that AI is a failure in the sense that to this day it has been impossible to build machines that have the understanding and common sense of a four-year-old. Certainly when compared with other successful scientific and engineering programs, such as the green revolution, the Apollo Moon landing, and organ transplantation, to name a few, AI is a failure.

The hubris of AI's quest for machines that think has been paralleled to a great extent by the quest for machines that teach. The latter quest has also been an enterprise starting out with great promise, and likewise has led to impressive results in limited domains. Both quests share a common anthropomorphic genesis, although the latter has had a far greater societal impact in terms of the allocation of public resources.

Many of the unsolved problems encountered by the two quests are common, so it would not be surprising to see their ultimate fates linked. What remained of the heroic attempts to rescue AI may be characterized as attempts to create machines that can learn, as a step on the way to making them think. The very popular and well-publicized field of neural nets has spearheaded this effort. This has been cognitive AI's last refuge.

Neural nets imitate the circuitry of the brain by having a collection of interconnected nodes, each of which has associated a numerical weight. The nodes respond to impulses, and their weights change over time. The neural net is said to "learn" by adapting to a given set of impulses.

There have been interesting and very useful "spin-offs" from the investigation of neural nets. But again, what has resulted is the familiar pattern of initial great expectations; the creation of professional societies and journals devoted to the furtherance of the technology, some impressive demonstrations, followed by stagnation and decline.

Technology has a way of advancing in unpredictable ways. This is particularly true when it comes to finding applications. Neural nets were a failure at developing cognitive AI, but a success in several other areas: object recognition in photographs, forecasting of financial markets, and adaptive noise abatement systems to name a few.

The expert system concept, born of AI technology, has seen success in certain areas. An expert system is a computer program designed to act somewhat like a human expert in some area of knowledge such as medical diagnosis, mineral prospecting, or corporate auditing. The program contains rules of inference together with a data base of domain facts all gleaned from none other than a real human expert in a specialized area.

Creating machines that teach requires solutions of a set of problems similar to that needed to create machines that learn. Therefore, our hope for the success of the former endeavor should be shaken by the failure to achieve the latter.

We can gain further insight into the shortcomings of cognitive AI from the recent experience of Japan. Consistent with a strong belief in the capability of computers to teach, the Japanese also bought-in heavily to the AI myth[77]. Launched in 1981, the Fifth Generation Project was a massive Japanese investment in "Good Old-Fashioned AI" or cognitive AI. This project had more to do with socioeconomic issues than with scientific. The socio-economic motivation came from a desire to build computers capable of recognizing and representing the numerous and complicated set of kanji characters. Reflecting similar efforts in the West, the Fifth Generation Project expended much capital but bore little fruit. It was officially declared dead on June 1 1992.[47]

Some might naively argue that the present generation of computers already has sufficient ability to think and therefore to teach as well. They run complex programs and solve problems, don't they? It is true that computers can teach, but what they teach are the principles of the machine: keyboard skills, how to use a spreadsheet, programming, etc. The naive argument continues, "Well, what's wrong with that?" The answer is that more basic skills including problem solving get pushed to the bottom of the pile. In fact, these are skills the computer is least capable of addressing.

How do we know this? One way is by the many examples of individuals with highly developed computer skills but with woefully inadequate basic skills: the skill to write a coherent English sentence, the skill to add numerical fractions, and the skill to understand vocabulary and use grammar correctly. A second way is by the fact that student achievement test scores have not increased (more often they have decreased!) since the introduction of computers in the classroom.

From the East to the West children are increasingly exposed to computers. Most love the interactive displays, games, and even the educational software. The story of Lewis[61], a fourteen year-old ninth grader, hired by Logo Computer Systems as a consultant to talk to educators interested in learning more about computers, casts doubt on the sanguine view of the role of computers in education.

Although not obsessed with computers, Lewis was nevertheless a virtuoso at the computer keyboard. To adults less familiar with computers, Lewis appeared a genius, almost able to work magic with the computer programs he was capable of writing. Unfortunately, this was not the whole story. In fact, Lewis, while in the ninth grade, was reading at only the fifth-grade level, and by his own admission, was a slow student.

While Lewis' story may be somewhat unusual, it is not unique. It does, however, clearly illustrate that basic skills, such as reading, are not automatically acquired as a consequence of the acquisition of computer skills. On the other hand, it does not deny the many justifiable uses and tremendous value of computers in our modern world. It's just that they don't do everything. It might be said that they think, but they certainly can't teach us how to think.

Unfortunately, the utility that computers have in teaching mathematics has been vastly overestimated, and consequently scarce resources have been squandered. Furthermore, it is very likely the case that computers have limited value in teaching many other subjects as well. Rather, they tend to siphon off valuable mental energy and divert scarce educational resources.

The principle that computers have limited instructional value may have exceptions for a very small group of students near the bottom in academic achievement (to give a figure, say, the lowest 5%) and, perhaps, for an even smaller group of students at the very top in academic achievement and ability. For the lowest achievers computer games and flashy graphics can function as attention grabbers and possibly help bring the lowest academic achievers, those who would probably otherwise be out on the street, some measure of participation in school.

At the opposite extreme, for the small percentage of exceptional students, already firmly grounded in the basics, the computer can either provide confirmation of mathematical intuition or else can be a means by which ideas generated quite apart from the computer find implementation.

It's a failing of human nature that we ascribe more to computer technology than it is capable of delivering. We can program computers to produce series of numbers, to draw interesting graphs and attractive geometric figures, and to make letter or paper writing infinitely easier. So why can't we use them to teach us mathematics as well? That we can seems a logical conclusion to draw, and it is certainly the one that has been drawn by a great many people in recent years. These same people have spent a great deal of the scarce resources available to the elementary and secondary schools on computers in the classroom.

These resources would have been infinitely better spent on almost anything else: musical instruments, library materials, art supplies, playground and sports equipment, not to mention salaries for teachers. If indeed, computers are on such a list, they should be very near the bottom. The proper place of computers should be in the teaching of keyboard skills and imparting a certain "computer awareness" to the students so that when they are encountered later in life, they are not feared and can be used for the purposes they were intended: word processing, spread-sheet making, and, yes, even computing.

Why teach a sixth-grader how to use a spreadsheet program? (One parent actually suggested this at a recent PTA meeting I attended.) It's not at all like learning to play the clarinet. Although there may be no harm in it, there's no virtue in learning such a work-specific and limited skill early in life, especially when there are other pursuits better suited to acquiring basic skills.

The computer age has rushed upon the industrialized world like no other revolution in history. We are in the process of defining computers, their many roles, their interaction with other machines, and indeed their place in our society. We are in a long period of experimentation with computers. It is to be expected that not all of these trials will end in success, at least initial success, and in fact it should not be too surprising to find that many of these experiments have had disastrous consequences.

Idiotic though it sounds, the claim has even been made that computers in the classroom can remove any need whatsoever for learning manipulative skills (for example, all of the arithmetic operations) or facts readily accessible by the computer. In other words, one's skills and knowledge reside in that box over in the corner. Furthermore, if my box is bigger and more powerful than your box, then so are my skills and memory. This is the concept of computer as mental prosthesis, correcting for mental inability as, for example, a hearing aid might correct for deafness.

Herbert Simon, a leading AI researcher, has made this view explicit[7] by suggesting that the meaning of the word "know" is changing from "having information stored in one's memory" to "the process of having access to information." This attitude is in many ways a logical extension of the role that computers and hand-held calculators play in many classrooms in this country. Learning arithmetic has been reduced to learning the correct keys to punch, or the correct buttons to push, to arrive at the correct answer.

CHAPTER 3

COMPUTERS IN THE CLASSROOM

Go out to almost any school in rural Montana and the chances are good you'll find old ghost computers: Ataris, IBM PC Juniors, Commodore-64s. These machines have been sitting around unused since they were purchased almost twenty years ago, when schools first bought-in to the computer literacy theme.

These were expensive machines, the modems alone cost about $500 at the time. They really couldn't do much, and there was very little software for them, and so they have sat unused all these years.

Those who have hyped computer skills as a substitute for basic skills have sold our nation a bill of goods. As a nation, spending on computers for schools topped the $2 billion level before the end of 1988[11]. That same $2 billion could have been used to hire an additional 20,000 teachers! How many additional teachers could have been hired with money spent on school computers since that time? Go figure.

As early as 1985 a survey by Market Data Retrieval Incorporated showed that at least fifteen thousand of the nation's one hundred thousand elementary and secondary schools were using microcomputers as teaching tools. At that time there was one computer for approximately every 125 students. Today the ratio is about one computer for every 9 students[84]. Sally Bowman Alden, executive director of the Computer Learning Foundation, thinks the ratio should be closer to the business average, which is one computer for every five employees.

The purchase of computers for schools is an easy call for school administrators and teachers alike. It's a lot easier to order a dozen Macs than to draw up a meaningful curriculum. It's also less controversial. Administrators, under pressure to hold costs down, order PCs instead of hiring new teachers and making upgrades to facilities.

In the rush to computerize the classroom, a great deal of time and money has been utterly wasted with little to show for the effort. Certainly as a result of the recent tremendous usage of computers in the classroom, many students have acquired computer skills. The trouble is that these skills are not the basic skills targeted (or that should be targeted).

Basic skills should be taught instead of the so-called computer skills. By this I mean the ability to do arithmetic with whole numbers as well as with fractions, and a grasp of the meaning and consequences of the basic laws of arithmetic. I would also include the ability to think through one and two-step problems and to make numerical estimations.

Even more damaging is the illusion that learning has taken place, and therefore real progress can be ignored. The worst instance of this thinking is the exhortation that, "I don't need to know all that junk (for example, the multiplication tables or the laws of commutativity and associativity), I can always work it out on my computer," or even worse, "My computer can work it out."

These declarations, as outrageous as they might seem, are not entirely without logic. We have accepted that machines have made it unnecessary to learn how to make the utensils we eat with, or how to milk a cow, or even how to do certain kinds of thinking. Some might, for example, include learning how to spell in the latter category.

Almost from the beginning it was observed that children took very quickly to computers, in many cases their knowledge surpasses that of their adult teachers. Brod[9] and others have viewed this leveling of the differences between the generations as unhealthy. In particular, heavy involvement with computers can encourage the child to put off dealing with the normal problems and conflicts of adolescence. Also, even though hand-eye coordination is necessary for keyboard/mouse manipulation, children who stop playing physical games such as soccer and basketball in favor of sitting in front of a video terminal begin to lose these very same motor skills.

The "gimmick argument," supporting the use of computers in the classroom, is frequently dismissed. This is the claim that the computer acts as a super-duper visual aid, an attention and interest grabber, especially if it's one of the newer multi-media kind with sounds as well as sights. The initial popularity, if not success, of computers in the classroom stems from the computer's ability to capture the interest of the intellectually turned-off child, the child bored with school and not doing well.

There are many such children in America's inner cities, and the computer may well play a role in saving such children from abject failure. Even though money for education is often scarce in the inner city, it does seem that extreme measures are required to get these children back on track. This argument does not apply, however, to the vast middle group of students who are positioned to learn the basic skills they need to advance academically.

Certainly computers can and do entertain children and adults of all ages. The games and the graphics are intricate, colorful, and kaleidoscopic. These benefits and the ability to make the computer perform these feats, however, should not be confused with learning basic skills or even with just plain learning.

It is perhaps understandable, if not forgivable, that computers and calculators have been looked to for salvation in the face of general deterioration of results in classrooms across the country. After all, technology has improved the quality of life and uplifted us in other areas. Why should this not also apply to the teaching of our children?

The following excerpt from a recent U.S. Department of Education publication[39] summarizes the heart of the argument advocating the use of computers and calculators in the teaching of mathematics:

"Calculators, computers, and related technology used as tools in the teaching and learning of mathematics transform the learner from calculator to critical thinker. Technology implies a shift from using brainpower for computational tasks to using brainpower to think critically, to communicate clearly, to solve mathematical problems, and to apply mathematics to complex scientific and social problems. Research shows that the proper use of calculators and computers can in fact enhance mathematics learning at all stages. *Calculators and computers can take the drudgery out of mathematics by handling routine arithmetic and algebraic calculations, freeing the learner to concentrate on the problem that requires such calculations.* (*Italics are mine*) Calculators and computers can be used to illustrate mathematical concepts graphically and this kind of visual representation can help understanding. Computers can simulate a variety of modeling options, freeing the learner to determine the most appropriate model to use in a given application."

The principal flaw in the above argument is that it is precisely the *drudgery of handling routine arithmetic and algebraic calculations*, i.e., the basic skills needed to do the mathematics, that the computer or calculator bypasses. The great majority of students need to learn those routine arithmetic and algebraic skills. The idea that bypassing these skills is somehow desirable is the basic folly.

The second mistake in the argument is the assumption that having bypassed the routine arithmetic and algebraic calculations, the student is then free to concentrate on problem concepts. The claim is not that the computer helps at the conceptualization stage, it is that it "frees the student." Any student unable to perform the routine calculations will not be aided at the conceptualization stage by being so freed.

It should be a matter of common sense to most who have encountered mathematics problems in school that the difficulty most often lies not in the execution but rather in the conceptualization. My sixth-grade daughter often says: "I know how to do the problem, I just don't know which number to divide into which." What she means of course, is that she can perform the required operations, it's just that she doesn't know which operations are required in what order.

It's important to note in passing that mathematicians at the Department of Education are as rare as hen's teeth. The author of the publication cited above was the only employee of that department at the time trained to the level of the doctorate. That fact alone is almost unbelievable. Why should mathematicians be so poorly represented among the thousands of employees of a cabinet level department of the United States Government?

Unfortunately, direction from the U.S. Department of Education has been heeded by more than a few high-school teachers and administrators. A recent Washington Post article[59] is about the large-memory graphing calculators that are required instruments in many schools. "It's essential that kids have one of their own," said Irving Stern, chairman of the math department at Wilson High School. His school purchased 80 of them at $80 a unit. It seems clear to all; the kids love the little machines.

Among the teachers, even the strong supporters of the calculators have noticed the game playing and the goofing off, not to mention their dishonest use in sometimes cheating on exams, such as history, that requires only memory. Nevertheless, when it comes to justification of the little devices, all the supporters know the party line, as Julie Jarrad, a senior at Watkins Mill says, "It takes a lot of the calculating and arithmetic out of [math]. There is less memorization, and they are teaching us to apply the concepts."

What? Did I hear that right? Let me repeat it: "It takes a lot of the calculating and arithmetic out of [math]." My God! What else is there to math? I know the answer to that; I'm a mathematician. Calculating and arithmetic are the HEART and SOUL of math!

Ms. Jarrad's statement is completely in line, indeed a paraphrase of the official Department of Education proclamation. The claim that "concepts" are being learned is bogus. The "concepts" that are being learned are not concepts of abstract algebra or even of basic arithmetic. They are the "concepts" of programming the calculator to achieve a desired response. Unfortunately, the educators themselves often do not understand the difference. Nevertheless, it is important to realize that these concepts are not the same.

Why not then, you might ask, be satisfied with teaching the concepts necessary to program the calculator, even if they are perhaps somewhat different from these other concepts? To the uninitiated it would seem that the graphing calculator's concepts are no less valid, and certainly they seem to be neither less complicated nor less extensive. A clue to one answer lies in the last line of the Post article. It is a quotation from Kathy Truesdale, a spokeswoman for Texas Instruments Inc., which makes one of the most popular models. "I guess this is the year for the graphing calculator." Next year what will it be? Having learned to program this year's model will undoubtedly make it easier to program whatever comes up next year.

Nowhere is the shortcoming of the computer and calculator more evident than it is when it comes to the estimation of numerical quantities. Indeed, the whole point of making an estimation is often a check on whether the machine is returning a correct answer. The ability to estimate is, or at least should be, a targeted basic skill. A very large percentage of day-to-day decisions based on numbers, which are exact by definition, are just as easily based on estimations of those numbers.

Learning to program a calculator will not teach students how to estimate numerical quantities, a skill at least as important as learning how to calculate precisely. Intelligent consumers as well as engineers have an ongoing need to make rapid numerical estimations. Numerical exactness is not always needed to make a decision on which item to purchase or what design to build, especially when these choices are limited. By definition the calculator has no role in making such estimation. The estimation is itself a numerical "check" on the calculator's result.

As Siegal and Markoff[61] have noted, the notion that computer literacy is rapidly becoming an economic necessity is misguided. Learning to program computers may give some youngsters the opportunity to move into well-paying programming jobs, and many will need computer skills in other endeavors. But both computers and the nature of computer skills are changing and will continue to change. Professional jobs of the future will require a general competence in verbal communication and mathematical reasoning. Today's specialized computer skills are certain to be superseded or outmoded by the demands of tomorrow's systems.

Calculators and computers make it even more imperative that the individual using them understand the fundamentals of arithmetic and be able to perform such operations, although perhaps not as rapidly as the machine. Imagine the opportunities for disaster created by an accountant, engineer, or even store clerk unable to do simple arithmetic but only able to punch the buttons on a machine!

The author John Paulos coined the word "innumeracy," the numerical equivalent of illiteracy[50]. Calculators and computers do not alleviate the problem of innumeracy; they circumvent it by always giving an answer. They act as a crutch on which the innumerate can persist in their ignorance. Innumerates, who almost always eschew mathematical reasoning, are the first to pull out their calculators when confronted with a problem.

Over the years, it has never ceased to amaze me how advanced and proficient a computer programmer can become, while having only a very superficial grasp of the underlying concepts. By this I mean the real concepts that would enable him to solve a different problem and then to tell another programmer how to use that same language to write a similar-looking program.

To observe a really good programmer plying his trade, the uninitiated is often deeply impressed with his technical skills. It would appear that the programmer has a profound grasp of "concepts." It is a serious mistake, however, to assume that these concepts are the root concepts needed for problem solving in a general context. In general, programmers are low on the corporate totem pole, and a programmer typically aspires to be promoted out of that role to a position requiring broader knowledge.

This strongly suggests that computer usage in the classroom, particularly by elementary school children, is of dubious value and is more likely to distract and detract from the development of basic skills.

The same remark extends to hand-held calculators. When a child is engaged in punching the keys on the computer or the buttons on a calculator, learning the material, which is presumably the point of the exercise, stops, or at the very least is seriously curtailed. This is because conceptualizing stops; the child's attention is focused on the "thing" and is miles removed from the intended idea.

It really couldn't be otherwise. The child is being asked to perform two tasks simultaneously, one of which, the learning, simply must have his undivided attention. In fact, not surprisingly, what the child is learning is... how to punch the keys on a computer or the buttons on a calculator and thereby achieve some end result on the screen or on the display.

Consider the task of memorizing the multiplication tables. Even most of the motor reinforcement that comes from painstakingly writing out a multiplication expression by hand is lost while tapping at the keyboard. Computers and calculators are of no help at all in developing an intuitive understanding of numbers and how they behave under the standard operations of addition, subtraction, multiplication, and division. This is the same intuition that is used to make intelligent numerical estimates.

Furthermore, the gross deficiency of the computer as a principal teaching tool runs deep and is not correctable by any conceivable means. There is no better software or faster computer that will set matters straight and transform the machine into even a shadow of what is expected of it.

One might say that perhaps it's the keyboard that's distracting. Replace the keyboard, for example, with direct voice control to the computer. Could this improvement make a difference in how the computer is used, say, to teach arithmetic skills? In this configuration the computer is now a fancy "flash card" server.

Now, most agree that flash cards are a useful tool in hammering home the multiplication tables, but probably are not more than a device or "prop." What possible advantage would the usual computer with keyboard-input have in this regard over the use of an equivalent set of the usual flash cards? Even flash cards would be less intrusive on the thought processes that must be mastered. Those, including the present author, who would dare to characterize the computer in the classroom as a "thousand dollar flash card" are considered hardened skeptics by some educators such as Seymour Papert.

In the absence of evidence that computers significantly advance the learning process, one frequently hears the claim: "At least the computer has a value as an attention grabber and serves to generate enthusiasm in otherwise disinterested students." This argument perhaps has some merit, particularly as it applies to students doing very poorly for whatever reason and unable to make progress via the traditional avenues. Such students very likely spend several hours each day sitting in front of a television screen. The computer screen could conceivably act as a bridge to something other than the utterly passive universe that stupefies and consumes so many hours.

What is commonly meant by "computer literacy" in reality implies a high-tech form of vocational training. As a subject it is neither science nor art, but is a skill whose value in the market place can be ephemeral. Most students could do a lot worse than become "computer literate." That's about as far as the argument can be pushed, however. If any real learning (and by this I mean learning such things as multiplication tables and how to think) is to take place, it must necessarily be in the mind of the student and take place quite apart from the computer.

One of the seemingly solid claims in favor of using computers in the classroom is that students will be forced to write correct English sentences. If the student is composing and sending messages, as for example over the Internet, this would seem to encourage writing. If computers are not able to teach mathematics, can students at least learn to write using them?

The answer is yes and no. First, there is no evidence that writing skills have improved among students using computers. The same ungrammatical sloppy English is simply purveyed via e-mail messages. The burden of proof should be on those who make the claim that writing skills can be improved directly as a result of using a computer. They should justify the expenditures of scarce resources to purchase hardware and software.

However, for those students at the very bottom in academic achievement, those who are marginally literate, using a computer could force them into at least functional literacy. But so could many other activities, such as sitting down with paper and pencil and writing letters.

What is the primary impetus behind the push to place computers in the classroom? The answer is mainly the parents of the children themselves. Supporting pronouncements by educators, computer manufacturers, and pundits in favor of the cause facilitate and lend legitimacy to the purchases. But more often than not, it's the well-meaning parents working through parent-teacher organizations who are the galvanizing force responsible for initiating and implementing the introduction of computers into the curriculum.

I recently attended a PTA meeting where the most frequently asked question of the teacher was: "What are you doing to make use of computer resources in teaching my child?" Commonly held beliefs, no matter how false or recent their origin, are difficult to dispel. An example is the belief, expressed by many of the parents attending that PTA meeting, that the mere presence of copious and expensive computer resources in the classroom buys a superior academic environment and facilitates learning. Nothing could be further from the truth.

Indeed, at the conceptual level mathematics and computers have virtually nothing in common. It is a mistake to reason by analogy that a computer is to mathematics as, for example, a violin or trombone is to music.

Computer Citizenship

Siegel and Markoff[61] have suggested that what they term "computer citizenship" should replace "computer literacy" as the desired goal in the schools. What they mean by computer citizenship includes knowledge of fundamental computer applications such as electronic banking, graphics design, computerized inventory control, and perhaps word processing. It is neither necessary nor desirable that students learn applications beyond what is needed for their classwork. By the time they are ready to use their skills in the workplace, the techniques will have changed. It's important to remember that the market demands excruciatingly specific up-to-date skills. My knowledge of the computer language FORTRAN, while very useful five to ten years ago, has little market value today.

What is meant more generally by computer citizenship is the knowledge of social, political, environmental, and military implications of computer technology. This knowledge is needed, for example, to be able to evaluate the threat that computerized record systems pose to individual privacy and freedom. When parents visit the classroom and spend more time examining what the computer will do than what the teacher is teaching, they are demonstrating poor computer citizenship.

My twelve-year-old daughter, Emilie, is a sixth-grader at Chesterbrook Elementary School in McLean, Virginia. Chesterbrook is home to children of the upper-middle-class in the nationally ranked Fairfax school system. The PTA of Chesterbrook Elementary budgeted over $26 thousand for computers, software, and training for the 1994-95 school year. This amounted to a whopping 54% of all funds raised that year by the PTA through dues and various fundraising activities!

Chesterbrook Elementary's PTA is probably typical of other PTAs in similar neighborhoods around the country. What did the

PTA spend on buying new books, PE equipment, or improvements to the building and grounds? Don't even ask. The computer "buy" is such an easy call. Everybody thinks, "Well, yes, I certainly want my child to have access to the best and not to fall behind all those other kids getting them." Not a word of opposition from anybody.

If the PTA president, a very business-minded and officious looking individual, had proposed spending a similar sum on books, there would have been long and agonizing discussions about which books to buy, and whether to include any of the controversial books having to do with sex or lifestyles or whatever. He knows that the computer buy is easy. It takes care of over half of the money the PTA has to spend, and everybody will be happy. Not me, I know that the PTA has just thrown away over half its money.

Look elsewhere around the country, and you'll see the same thing going on. In Danville, Kentucky, Woodlawn Elementary's parent teacher organization acted to raise $130,000 to pay for a state-of-the-art computer system. The PTA was the galvanizing force responsible for initiating and implementing the multi-phase plan. Kentucky Education Technology funds will contribute another $60,000 to the effort. Ultimately, Woodlawn envisions a network of over 200 computers throughout the school campus.

What will they get for the money? When students return to school in September, they will be using a 27-station computer network running Computer Curriculum Corp.'s multimedia educational software, SuccessMaker. An ad for the software boasts, "The self-paced computer instruction integrates reading, math and science modules to create an individualized learning experience for each student."

There is a growing body of research that shows little or no difference in the success rates of students taught with or without them. "Computer-based teaching is just like radio, film and the television before it," said sociologist David Livingstone[13], who teaches at the Ontario Institute for Studies in Education. "There is a mass of hoopla, but research shows there is little really accomplished." Low-tech techniques, says Livingstone, have the huge benefit of "being cheaper."

Fortunately, not every school has bought in to the extent of Woodlawn Elementary. In fact, with evidence piling up that the money would have been better spent on more teachers or supplies, a trend is starting in the other direction.

It is not surprising then to see the very same parents becoming disillusioned with the effectiveness of computers in the classroom and now demanding a return to "basics[81]."

In fact, the jury is starting to come in on the question of whether computers contribute to boosting test scores. And the jury is bringing back the unanimous verdict that they do not. Take the case of the Christopher Columbus middle school in Union City, N.J. Even President Clinton and Vice President Gore have toured its expensive and highly touted computer facilities.

Test scores among its 300 previously low achieving students have soared in recent months. Surely, you say, this must be an example in favor of the effectiveness of computers in the classroom. Some admiring onlookers and even news stories said that a partnership with Bell Atlantic Corporation, which helped stuff the schoolrooms with computer equipment, was the catalyst in effecting the rise.

The example of the Christopher Columbus School is now rightly regarded as a myth[76f]. Educators now say that what actually produced the startling rise in test scores were new books, after school programs to help with homework, and a sweeping reform of the curriculum. At best, it might be said that the computers made attending school more attractive, since most of the students at Christopher Columbus school do not have a computer at home.

Even the people purveying information technology to schools acknowledge that their efforts have produced no payoff.[25] Among this group and educators alike there has always been an expectation that the next 18 to 24 months would bring revolutionary change in how people teach and learn. The information technologists have noted the swelling educational budgets over the last 25 years and the sagging student performance. They attribute the former to administrative overhead (certainly not to the vast sums that went into their own pockets), but are dumbfounded at the latter.

The placing of computers in the classroom is an international phenomenon. Some countries have bought in more than others have. In Australia the computer-student ratio is about 1:19; that's low when compared to the 1:9 US ratio. In Holland, which has been slower due to financial reasons, the ratio is only 1:70.

As one might expect, the Japanese have led the way in placing computers in the classroom. In Japan, over 50 percent of the elementary schools have personal computers, 86 percent of junior high schools, and 99 percent of senior high schools have them[69].

Recently[82] a panel of experts advising the Japanese education minister on multimedia said that every student at a state school, local government school or university should have access to a personal computer by the turn of the century. The aim should be according to the panel to have **one personal computer per student.**

CHAPTER 4

COMPUTERS IN THE CLASSROOM: EDUCATORS' APPROACHES

Early pioneers in the field of computer instruction certainly felt the coming of a revolution in the classroom. In speaking of computer literacy one such educator, Alfred Bork[5] notes that "In dealing with change, purchasing, maintaining bankbooks, to be able to perform simple arithmetic, or to use devices which perform it, is essential. *A person who cannot do arithmetic is at a distinct disadvantage in our society; but this is changing as calculators and computers become more common."*

The implication of this is that the use of calculators and computers will erase the disadvantage of the person unable to do arithmetic, as, for example, the invention of eyeglasses has erased the disadvantage of the nearsighted. Nothing could be further from the truth.

Eyeglasses correct for nearsightedness because, except for a single component of the vision system, namely the lens, all else is presumed in working order. A calculator or computer does not correct for the inability to perform arithmetic, because this inability implies that there are almost certainly deficiencies in other areas, primarily in number intuition.

Imagine an accountant or an engineer without an underlying grasp of arithmetic and mathematics and who is at the mercy of a calculator. What if he punched in a wrong number, would his intuition alert him to this happening? Unless he is following a cookbook, how will he know what numbers to enter into the calculator? Does the order of the calculator's operations matter? How would he ever know about the accuracy of his answer?

The history of computers is short enough, and the history of the personal computer is even shorter. At the risk of oversimplification we shall divide the history of educators' approaches to computers in the classroom into two branches: early CAI approaches and modern, usually multimedia, approaches. Despite receiving widespread criticism, the CAI branch continues to the present as the dominant mode of computer classroom instruction. Our first example comes from early CAI. We begin by examining Alfred Bork's book based on papers written during the 1970's and reflecting the work of the Physics Computer Development Project and the Educational Technology Center at the University of California, Irvine.

The introductory overview is notable for its sanguine prophecies: "We are at the brink of a major revolution in ways of learning... The revolution will occur within the next 25 years and will affect our educational system at all levels." The author goes on to trace the history of human learning in a way that is now familiar:

- oral tradition and interaction with other humans
- written documentation and the lecture
- development of printing and the textbook
- The (you guessed it!) COMPUTER.

As evidence of the coming distinguished role of the computer in learning, Bork cites what he considers the best examples of computer-aided instructional material. This he claims makes the learning process an "...active process, where students play a constant thinking role." Furthermore, individual students can control the pace of learning, backtrack and review material, etc., all of which is impossible in the traditional classroom situation. The clincher for the author is that the cost of computers, while perhaps high at that moment, is coming down by about 30% each year.

As if all of these prognostications are not breathtaking enough, Bork predicts that "...computers will soon be more important in our educational process than books, and, indeed, may entirely replace the book medium for many purposes." These grandiose predictions paralleled and echoed similar ones made by AI researchers, particularly Marvin Minsky head of the AI project at MIT.

It seems fair to say that Bork's predictions at the time were mainstream and, indeed, if the tone has since become less strident, these views continue to be widely held by many educators.

Twelve years later education theorists, especially those having an AI bent, will have discredited the computer-aided instructional material as a mistaken path off the revolutionary road. One leader of the AI approach was Seymour Papert of MIT. By the way, according to Bork, the revolution should have been about half completed at the time of Papert's writing.

Bork makes the distinction between computer-aided instruction based on a dialog with the student versus the computer as a page-turner. The former programs are more interactive, select paths through the material based on the students' responses, and provide the student with feedback. The latter programs simply present large chunks of text, asking intermittent questions ("TYPE 1 FOR YES, 0 FOR NO"), but do not vary the material presented significantly on the basis of the student's responses. Indeed, Bork offers that the educational value of such programs is questionable.

The mistake that Bork and others make is that, while the process appears to be "interactive," it is only so in the sense of the word used by computer scientists. In fact, the student's role as a learner has become more passive. He is constrained to take whatever paths the programmer intended him to take. This is an absolute limitation of the software.

Secondly, however the scenario is viewed, he is *reacting* to a visual display. While it may be true that reflective thinking is required to continue the "interaction" to achieve a desired response from the computer, the process itself detracts from self-originating thought. By self-originating thought, I mean something that is at the heart of the learning process, not just the memorization process.

There are several overlapping areas between the problems of traditional AI and computer learning. One of these is the area of cognitive psychology, which claims a wide following among learning theorists. Cognitive psychologists attempt to model ways that the brain organizes knowledge, and this is exactly one of the problems approached by AI. The cognitive approaches have promised much but have delivered little in terms of the software design of learning modules.

Most of the existing instructional software is modeled on the classical behavorialist philosophy: run the maze correctly and get a little cheese reward at the finish line. Programmed learning based on this approach breaks down the larger instructional tasks into bite-sized chunks. After mastering a little chunk, the student takes a test and is rewarded with praise, advancement to the next chunk, etc.

Although initially overly optimistic about the future of computers in learning, Bork's book[5] contains some caveats and solid observations. The first is that, given the increasing number of learners confronted by our educational system, the networked computer at least has the capacity to serve the coming multitudes.

Also, the nature of computer instructional software is reminiscent of the dialogue between student and teacher. As Bork notes, almost all educational psychologists agree that the optimum setting for education is the "one-on-one" dialogue between excellent teacher and student. He goes on to acknowledge that no existing software is capable of imitating the excellent teacher, the better examples can at least be approximations.

The conclusion of Bork's observations is clearly the following. What is needed, if the computer is to be up to the best Socratic standards, is that it pass what is known as Turing's test, i.e., that the computer perform *indistinguishably* from a real-life human, who happens to be an excellent teacher. One would think that this would require the computer candidate to pass at least some of the preliminary trials on the way to fulfilling the AI dream. For example, it should have the common sense of a four-year-old. As we have pointed out earlier, achieving even this seemingly modest goal is still out of reach today.

Existing software does not render its computer host capable of acting in the best Socratic sense. Nevertheless, assuming that we do have superlative educational software, is the end result really as good as the human teacher in a real classroom? Do we wish to spend our scarce resources on the necessary hardware and software as well as devote large amounts of precious time? I believe that the answer to these questions must be "no."

Given that the Turing test is met, there still remain important unanswered questions. The Turing test alone may not meet other important criteria. Does the software promote diversity in the material subjects? Would the students all come out knowing exactly the same things with the same degree of emphasis on each topic? Would a student be as motivated to learn with a machine teacher as he or she might for a human teacher?

Following the retreat of their AI colleagues, even the most diehard advocates for the computer as teacher have taken a fallback position. The computer becomes an adjunct device, one to be used in conjunction with the textbook and other traditional means, even the dreaded lecture. The latter is the thing the computer learning advocates argue most strongly against. They claim that the lecture offers the least interaction between student and teacher, and their remedy, the computer, offers a great deal of interaction.

I have always thought that the purpose of the lecture, particularly at the university level, is not so much to teach as it is to inspire, to point the way, to stimulate the student to learn for himself or herself. And the same is really true at the elementary level, although the lecture there is less formal and should be more like story telling and provide for dialogue with individual students in the classroom.

Richard Feynman's notes and books are valuable learning materials, but anyone who attended the famous physicist's lectures came away inspired. It may be a cliché that teachers are remembered for the inspiration that they bring to a subject long after the memory of detail fades, but it is nevertheless true.

At this point the advocates of computer learning are faced with the same reality as their AI colleagues. Everyone can see the familiar pattern of initial great expectations, a costly build up of infrastructure to support the program, some impressive demonstrations, followed by stagnation and decline. Most of the advocates for computer learning, including Bork and Papert have acknowledged that to date the dream has been unrealized, even if its fulfillment is just around the corner. Bork places the blame in two places:

- Not enough quality educational software available for extensive classroom use. (He states that this situation *may* change in the near future. One has a palpable sense of the diminution of the great initial expectations.)
- Few teachers have adequate knowledge of how to use computers in learning.

Bork has also identified social problems that have risen such as the advantage affluent families have in providing their children with machines. His prediction, however, that computer costs would correct this was wrong. The cost of a personal computer today is significant, even for a middle class family.

True, the cost of personal computers has come down in the sense that the money to buy a machine today having last year's capabilities is perhaps 50% less. But who wants last year's machine? Not even the poor. Besides, the new software probably won't run on it anyway.

The cost of this year's machine is not significantly less than last year's cost of last year's machine. Back in 1985 I paid $1,800 for an IBM PC clone. Twelve years later that's just about what I would pay today for a personal computer with current technology.

MODERN APPROACHES OF EDUCATORS

The most recent approach of educators to computer learning has been to acknowledge the shortcoming of traditional CAI while offering software with new wrinkles that purports to transform the computer into a valuable learning tool.

Seymour Papert's[49] approach was to return to the primary function of the computer, namely a machine to be programmed. His programming language *Logo* for children was designed to transform the computer into a "pencil" for the mind.

Instead of trying to teach content, Papert sets the very laudable goal of trying to get the kids "turned on" to learning. The actual learning itself should follow as a corollary. He attempts to reach his goal by means of a technique well known to mathematicians, the so-called *discovery process.* Following the method in a classroom setting, the teacher does no lecturing, but only poses questions and problems and gently guides the discussion.

In order that the discovery process work, the teacher's part must be carried out in a very careful, thoughtful manner, and members of the class must be brought in as full participants. First the questions are easy, but as answers pile up, the questions become more provocative. The teacher's job is not to give on-the-spot judgments to the students' answers, but rather to respond in a way that causes the student to reflect further.

If everything happens just right, lights go on and the student experiences the thrill of discovery. This can be a very satisfying and energizing experience, and indeed, far more valuable than learning mere facts. The discovery process has the further advantage that it can work well with students having almost no preparation or background.

Its drawbacks are that it is a time consuming process, and it does require a fairly astute teacher. The teacher must ask the right questions at the right time, give the right amount of encouragement, and in general know how to set things up so that the magic happens.

Papert's approach with his programming language Logo is to implement the discovery process. It is believable that his technique works to some extent. Logo is one of many instruments that could be substituted with the same effect. The results are best, however, when an effective human is substituted for the instrument.

Once I witnessed the performance of an exceptionally talented teacher running an elementary math class via the discovery method. The students were poor black inner-city kids. No computer programming language could have done half as good a job as that teacher did in getting the kids turned on to math and science.

While it is conceivable that a machine could play a passive role in the discovery method, it is more likely to be a distraction to the process of independent and creative thinking. Papert's approach, nevertheless, answered many of the objections to CAI, but if Logo does lead the student to learn how to think by programming, it does not address learning traditional basic skills. If the computer is to become more than a very minor adjunct to the educational process, it must at least do that.

Roger Schank and Chip Cleary[55] of the Institute for the Learning Sciences (ILS) at Northwestern University have taken a different and interesting approach. Taking a page from the book of aircraft simulation software, the ILS has developed *social simulation software*. This software claims to teach the student by forcing him to interact in simulated social environments.

One such module called *Dustin* (after Dustin Hoffman, the actor) is used for language instruction. The student is presented with a simulated scenario, such as a trip to the store to buy groceries or to the bank to apply for a loan. The student types his responses to the video image of the grocery clerk or the bank teller. If he gets it wrong, Dustin takes action by either showing examples of correct answers or else by breaking the task down into smaller easier to handle tasks. The student can ask the video image to repeat itself any number of times, and he has access to on-line aids such as a dictionary.

The social simulation software is certainly a clever idea. Simulation software is successful in training pilots, astronauts, and even physicians who want to learn how to perform some tricky operation. But the point of that software is that it saves risking lives and expensive equipment. All things being equal, it would certainly be better to train on the real thing.

What does the social simulation software save or offer as an advantage? Clearly there is nothing to be saved, except possibly for the time of the flesh and blood people who would teach the student. Of course, that saving comes at the expense of the hardware and software performing the simulations. Is it an advantage to be able to avoid real-life encounters or even classroom encounters acting out what the software is simulating? As novel as it is, this approach is not applicable to the learning of subjects other than those related to language and social skills.

CHAPTER 5

COMPUTERS AND INTUITION

The human race suffered an historic defeat this year, or perhaps it was an historic victory. Playing to "defend our [human] dignity," world chess champion Garry Kasparov was defeated in the last game by IBM's Deep Blue RS/6000 SP computer in New York City. Last year Kasparov defeated Deep Blue 4 games to 2. But last year Deep Blue was using only brute force; that is, little strategy was built into its program. It only blindly checked the millions of possible moves, and made the one having the highest "score." Before this year's match, however, Deep Blue went to chess school. It (he/she?) has been given some intuition, meaning that rules have been added to its programming that allow it to narrow its choices. It now knows, and has no trouble remembering, strategies already thought out by its human creators.

Kasparov, said that he could "feel [Deep Blue's] intuition" in last year's games. Even chess experts reflected that one of Deep Blue's games was very "human." But for the most part, Blue is still relying on its advantage in being able to check two hundred million moves in one second. Kasparov can perhaps check two moves in the same second! Blue has a hundred million to one advantage in that department. The fact that the match was so close is testament to Kasparov's brilliant intuitive play. A hundred-million-to-one advantage is difficult to overcome.

Since we can't rely on Deep Blue's brute force method, intuition must be a key ingredient in human learning. That is one reason to question the teaching role of computers and calculators. Intuition is simply not one of their strong qualities, at least today. Learning arithmetic, for example, requires developing a certain intuition about numbers; it is not just about memorizing the multiplication tables or how to extract the square root. The computer or calculator does not aid in developing this intuition; indeed, it can work against it.

Intuition about a subject implies an indefinable feeling or sense for its elements. It is in part the ability to make associations. This is what is known in AI as "chaining." In mathematics, and probably other fields as well, this is done sometimes consciously and sometimes unconsciously. The art of association lies at the heart of making new discoveries. Intuition has other facets as well, notably the ability to reason by analogy. In fact, this logically comes after associations have been made.

There are three different types of thinking that people do when it comes to numbers. The first type, numerical estimation, is intuition based. The second type, exact numerical calculation, is what computers and calculators do best. The third type, theorizing about numbers, is intensely intuitive. Computers and calculators have very little utility in the first and third types of thinking. There is yet a fourth type of reasoning that binds all three together, namely logic, which we will have more to say about later.

Let's consider numerical estimation. A competent consumer is constantly faced with the need to quickly arrive at numerical estimates; the exact amount is rarely needed to make a decision. Do I have enough money in my wallet for a trip to Philadelphia and back? Should I elect the $200 deductible over the $500 deductible auto insurance policy and pay $57 dollars more per year?

The judge dismissed a recent court case. The reason given was that no one in the courtroom had a calculator to determine how many feet the defendant's car traveling at 40 miles per hour would have moved in one second! Could the defendant's car have possibly passed through the intersection in a mere second?

Since someone in the courtroom must have had a pencil, and someone else must have known that there are about 5,000 feet in a mile, I doubt that a calculator would have made any difference. Knowing how to proceed and only sixth grade arithmetic would have sufficed to produce an estimate. The defendant's car could have easily cleared the intersection in one second!

And what about refinancing the mortgage on my house? Rates are down one-and-a-half percentage points, but I will pay a finance fee of fifteen hundred dollars and two points for the first year. How many years will it be before I am ahead? Of course, if I am unable to estimate the outcomes myself and rely on advice of the mortgage broker, he's almost certain to tell me to go ahead and refinance.

Packages of two bars of soap sell for 59 cents; a package of three for 88 cents, which to buy? If I choose wrong, paying an extra fraction of a penny certainly won't hurt, but what if more money were at stake as it often is?

"Why not just whip out the calculator?" you say. Assuming that I have remembered to bring my calculator with me to the store, the answer is that I don't need or even want an exact answer. A VERY fastidious person with a calculator might divide 59 cents by 2 to get 29.5 cents cost per bar for the two-soap package and divide 88 cents by 3 to get 29.33 cents cost per bar for the three soap package. Most people expect that the cost per bar is less for the larger package. Verifying this should not take a calculator. Three packages of the two per pack soap would cost $1.77, whereas two packages of the three per pack would cost $1.76. That's right, buy the three soaps per package!

Once one has already developed an intuition about numbers, computers can sometimes provide a confirmation and reinforcement of it. They cannot engender intuition.

How could it be that computers might aid in developing numerical intuition? One might write a program that would cause, say, the prime numbers to scroll on the video screen. Would watching the numbers scroll by somehow be an aid to understanding the behavior of prime numbers? That would be less likely than learning to oil paint by attending museum exhibits. Of course, to write the program in the first place would require a certain understanding of the prime numbers, but that knowledge and intuition could not have been obtained from the computer.

It's significant that over two hundred years ago mathematicians who pored over printed pages of prime numbers first guessed the deepest theoretical facts about the prime numbers. A computer video screen, had it been available, could have been used in the same way, but the fact that deep numerical conjectures were made without the benefit of computers is proof that they were not in any way required.

On a computer it's impossible to tell the difference between a fraction and a number that's not a fraction. It's also impossible to tell whether a decimal goes on forever or terminates. There is a limit to the number of digits the computer is capable of using to represent any number. Does all of this matter? Certainly not when it just comes to getting an answer. An engineer needs a certain number of digits and that's it.

Intuition about numbers is not about "just getting an answer." Because the computer can hold only a certain number of digits, some digits on the tail are necessarily dropped and there is a "round-off error." Making this little error once or even a few times probably won't matter. But what if the little errors are made thousands of times? The little errors can add up to one big whopping error!

Concepts such as fractions and decimals that go on forever are critical to understanding how these errors accumulate and affect the final answer. An engineer who doesn't understand this and take appropriate corrective action is like an ape at the controls of a 747 jumbo jet.

Everyone has heard the cliché, "Don't believe everything you read." It should be expanded to read, "Don't believe everything that the computer prints out." Even more than the printed word, people tend to place blind faith in the numerical outputs of computers and calculators. Except for an occasional Pentium processor (a problem fixed long ago), computers don't make mistakes! True, but people entering numbers into these machines and writing their programs do. And the computers don't know the difference or even care.

And how do we catch these mistakes? First, we must rely on our intuition to know whether the answer is approximately correct. Secondly, we often need alternative ways to carry out the calculation as a check on the result of the first answer. Again, this step either involves intuition or knowledge probably not obtainable from the machine.

The rules of logic, which bind the three types of numerical thinking, must be learned in order to solve multi-step problems. It's surprising how many high-school students are unable to make a meaningful distinction between the statements: "If A then B," and "If B then A." So, for example, if A is known to be false, which of the last two statements imply that B is false as well?

Do computers teach logic? Unless you are learning a programming language, I don't see that they do. In fact, the very process of number crunching leaves all of the supporting logic up to the user. The computer does not interpret its results, which are always qualified and based on assumptions known only to the user.

Logic is at the base of understanding the mathematical operations being carried out. When measuring student accomplishments, it is also the easiest to overlook. It has to do with the old principle that just getting the correct answer is sometimes not enough. Take the example of students who have been taught to program their calculators to find the real number roots of a second-degree polynomial. The calculator obscures the logic, which determines whether there are two solutions, one solution, or no solutions. What does the flashing "E" mean when a certain sequence of numbers is entered? Was an incorrect button pushed? Does it possibly mean that there are no solutions, or are the batteries just running down?

The student merely enters a series of numbers into the calculator and sees a number come out (or the flashing "E.") It's the same with computers; you have inputs and outputs. It's always up to the user to interpret the results. Moreover, more often than not, programming does not force the student to reflect on the logic going on behind the scene. The machine does not "free" the student to reflect when he would otherwise not do so.

No one has suggested that computers be used to develop other intuitive skills. Can you imagine practicing the piano on the computer? I suppose you might learn musical nomenclature or about the history of music from CD ROMs, but you could never come to know the touch and feel of an instrument.

True, one might use modern techniques in virtual reality to learn procedural skills such as how to fly an airplane or how to perform a complex operation without going to the hospital. But these are tasks not based on intuition; or at least they should not be.

And what about art? There is such a thing as computer art, but it seems highly unlikely to achieve the status of classical sculpture or painting. Few would advocate the computer as an adjunct to acquiring or developing active artistic ability. The operative word in the last sentence is "active," since now, or at least soon, one will presumably be able to access via the Internet the treasures of many of the great museums of the world such as the Louvre.

CHAPTER 6

THE ROMANCE OF COMPUTERS

Long before its realization as a functioning machine, the computer has been romanticized. It has been touted as a "bicycle for the mind," and a "ship for the soul." Stories written for the very popular television series "*Star Trek*" center on the starship Enterprise's computers. Even one of the principal actors, Data, is himself a computer. And who can forget Hal, the ship's computer in the movie "2001: A Space Odyssey?" Admittedly, Hal got a bit out of hand and had to be euthanized.

People often relate to computers in anthropomorphic terms. Like humans they are subject to viruses. They have a brain (the CPU), memory, and at least a primitive voice. Moreover, the terminal screen itself has the frontal aspect of a human being, even if it is one-eyed. It is almost as if someone or something is staring back at the user. It was suggested that one reason for the lack luster commercial success of Apple's Lisa computer was its Neanderthal appearance. The Lisa's screen hung over its base reminiscent of Neanderthal's forehead.

NEANDERTHAL LISA

The iridescent computer monitor exercises a hypnotic trance on many users, particularly on children. It's easy to imagine falling into the machine like Alice fell into the rabbit's hole and into a world of adventure. The idea of falling into the machine and becoming part of its world is an old one in science fiction. The sci-fi movies *Virtuality* and *Tron* exploit this theme. The surreal world beyond is made up of electrons and kaleidoscopic light, and as in Alice's Wonderland world, the laws of physics are exciting and quite different from reality.

The proponents of the information superhighway have likened the computer to a vehicle whose wings are two navigational joysticks on each side, like a pilot's controls, allowing you to steer through an atmosphere of knowledge and learning[58]. The image that comes to mind is something like Aladdin's magic carpet carrying us off to exotic Arabian adventures.

Those who are most enthusiastic about the computer as a tool for education have romanticized the computer in a somewhat different way. Although they share the vision of a Knowledge Navigator with the information superhighwaymen, their vision is focused more on exploration. The exploration they envision may be that of an ecosystem on planet earth or it may be that of the inside of a living organism. Captain Nemo's vessel the Nautilus in Jules Verne's "Twenty Thousand Leagues under the Sea" comes to mind. The computer will make learning "fun" and stimulate the imagination so that students will begin to "think for themselves."

Many of these romantic visions of the computer are marketing ploys. Romance is a side benefit of purchasing and using the machine. As a marketing tool, however, romance has proven to be one of the better options, particularly when the utility of the product being marketed is difficult to define, or when it's difficult to differentiate the product from its competitors.

Cigarettes are a case in point. The Marlboro man, Uncle Joe Camel, and Humphrey Bogart movies have romanticized cigarette smoking to some extent. Romanticizing a product or brand name has created entire markets: women's lingerie, luxury automobiles, and perfumes to name a few.

The same principle has been applied to the marketing of PCs and software. Feelings of emotion and romance are elicited in the mind of the user of the product. Presumably, the PC user will share some of the same feelings that a real adventurer or explorer might experience as he glides into the never-never world of cyberspace.

It would seem to be a very radical idea, indeed, to reverse this process by attempting to put emotions **into the computer** instead of into the user. That's exactly what David Gelernter, a computer scientist at Yale, has advocated. He wants to put emotions (fake emotions, that is) into the computer, not for marketing purposes, but rather for the purpose of imparting creativity to the machine.

Professor Gelernter has advanced the interesting thesis that cognitive AI has failed because it has not taken into account a spectrum of mental focus that characterizes the human mind. The high end of the spectrum, or high-level focus, is characterized by analytical, logical, and emotionless thinking. As the focus knob is turned down, according to the theory, thinking becomes less focused and more dream-like. And as this happens, emotions become more important in the chaining of random thoughts. It is at this low-focus end that creativity finds its spark. Or so the theory goes.

Modern computers and software are not capable of changing focus and are certainly not capable of emotions. According to Gelernter emotion is the missing piece in the AI puzzle. "A computer that never hallucinates cannot possibly aspire to artificial thought[31]."

Therefore, the argument goes, a cognitive computer should be capable of emotion and metaphorical thought. The argument is made more plausible by the fact that much of creativity occurs at the lower-focus levels of thought. Gelernter is dead serious and has attempted to incorporate the human sense of emotion into AI computer programs. Mind you he does not believe that this is *real* emotion, only an attempt at making fake emotion.

Can you imagine a computer with mood swings, one who might wake-up (boot-up) on the wrong side of the bed (memory board)? A cognitive computer could be expected to have a personality like the now almost forgotten characters R2D2 and C3PO from the first of the "Star Wars" movie series.

In writing on the subject of the psychology of invention in mathematics, the famous French mathematician Jacques Hadamard[34] describes successive layers of consciousness. According to Hadamard, the spark of creativity follows a period of preparation and incubation and its coming is marked not necessarily by wide-awake consciousness, but more often by a state of relaxation sometimes dream-like. The optimal state for creativity that Hadamard describes is not complete unconsciousness, but it is, nevertheless, a long way from full alertness. Gelernter would say that the "focus knob" is turned down during that period.

Hadamard tells the story of a mathematician who took advantage of this principle by deliberately falling asleep in a chair while holding a stone over a bucket of water placed under the chair's arm. The spark of an idea would often come in that instant just before being awakened, as the stone would fall.

EMOTION AND LEARNING

Most memory mnemonics are based on chaining or association. We are taught that the best way to remember a name is to associate something related to it. Many years ago my dad showed me how to do this when my sixth-grade school assignment was to memorize all of the state capitols. Through the association method I was easily able to memorize each of the capitol cities in a single evening. With some practice this can be a skill useful beyond the classroom. You can remember the name of Mr. Fish, whom you met at a party last night, because you imagined his rather flat face to be like that of a flounder.

Intense human emotion associated with an occurrence usually crystallizes the memory of the event. Those who have received traumatic news of the death of a friend or loved one can remember many years later the overwhelming wave of emotion and other non-related details that occurred at the time. Even less intense emotion imprints memory.

All human teachers show emotion to some degree. Students, particularly young students, are very receptive to visual and verbal cues that their teacher is broadcasting. The computer provides no emotional framework for the chaining of ideas to take place. If the concept of emotion as a facilitator of the "chaining" of ideas is correct, then it is reasonable to conclude that a flesh and blood teacher has an inherent advantage over a machine. Therefore, emotion may be one reason why a flesh and blood teacher is usually a better teacher than a machine.

CHAPTER 7

EDUCATIONAL SOFTWARE

Whatever classroom success the computer might claim depends upon the available educational software. To gain a better understanding of exactly what's available, it's useful to trace the development of this software over the past thirty years. Quite naturally, the evolution of any software is influenced by the capabilities of the machines on which it is run.

The initial programs were of the "page turner" type that allowed very little interaction with the student. The precursor of this instructional mode was the educational video popular in the schools in the 50's and 60's. Of course, that provided for no student interaction whatsoever, at least during the showing of the video.

The next generation software was more clearly recognizable as being in the computer-aided instruction (CAI) mold. That software has persisted as the most common and successful model in applications requiring memorization of a coherent set of facts by a mature student. Examples of this are:

- CAI for students learning the rules-of-the-road in order to obtain their drivers' licenses
- CAI for military recruits learning the components of a weapons system
- CAI for students learning to use a new word-processor system (this is more than just on-line help)
- CAI for arithmetic drill including multiplication tables.

The CAI software is not all of uniform quality. A great deal of it has a readily recognizable industrial quality, and almost all of it is written for the mature student capable of sitting through a rather extensive interactive dialog interspersed with diagnostic quizzes.

The cover of the recent book[48] by Seymour Papert features a glowing terminal against a backstop starry night. One expects the movie character ET to emerge from the mystical screen. The flyleaf summary accurately synopsizes the author's main contention: Computers haven't yet succeeded in revolutionizing learning, but this is because they are misunderstood and are not being properly utilized in the classroom. Nonetheless, Papert believes that we are poised on the threshold of a great advancement in learning. If we believe Bork we have been so poised for more than twelve years.

Somehow we are to deduce Papert's conclusions from anecdotal evidence provided by visionary teachers using computers to enrich learning. Papert's book is more about his educational philosophy than it is about computers as instruments of learning. Nevertheless, it certainly would seem that his book provides a glimpse of a concept that has failed and continues to fail.

His attempt to rescue the role of the computer as a tool in children's learning is muddled. At least Papert recognizes the failure of the computer as a learning tool as used in CAI. What miraculous alternative techniques will transform the beast into beauty? Perhaps if it's just integrated properly into the school environment and used in a very clever way, knowledge and learning will burst forth.

His Logo language for children is a valiant attempt to rescue some role for the computer in the education of children. Alas, Papert's wishful thinking does not lead him to the inevitable conclusion: the computer is certainly not capable of learning for the child, nor is it capable of teaching very much to the child.

The prototype of CAI software was developed beginning in 1963 by Patrick Suppes and Richard Atkinson at Stanford University. This was CAI for arithmetic drill. The computer generates random problems of a given type, say two digit multiplication, sequentially presents the student with the problems, keeps a running account of the student's performance, and advises when proficiency, as defined by either the human teacher or computer, has been attained. This basic software has been upgraded over the years, but it remains essentially unchanged. It has been the most commercially successful computer based learning material, and, moreover, tests by the Educational Testing Service[52] have shown that the system does have merit. Certain students' performances are improved significantly, particularly those starting near the bottom.

In 1967 Suppes and two associates founded a company, Computer Curriculum Corporation (CCC), which offers software drill and practice in the basic areas of mathematics, reading, and language arts. For the most part, CCC materials are used to help academically and economically disadvantaged students. Large urban school systems such as LA, Chicago, and Philadelphia have been heavy users of Suppes' system.

The math offerings range from first grade through high school. These packages and similar CAI software claim to be more than just programmed instruction. In fact, this latter term is eschewed in favor of jargon that emphasizes the enhanced interactive nature and added graphics capabilities of the software.

No review of CAI would be complete without mention of the Plato system developed in the early 1970's by Robert B. Davis, Donald Bitzer, and others at the University of Illinois. Plato was a time-shared based system using mainframe computers at the University and remote touch sensitive terminals around the country.

Plato followed Davis' Socratic interaction and discovery philosophy, and was fun for the kids to boot. Plato's three basic "strands" were:

- whole number arithmetic
- fractions, mixed numbers, and decimals
- graphs, variables, functions, and equations.

Some of the modules were more didactic than others, but the fun and games were mixed in and cleverly designed to exercise concepts set forth in the formal sessions and to avoid the boredom inevitable with straight CAI. The touch screen capability even allowed children with no keyboard skill access to Plato material.

The main difficulty with Plato was that its access to the general population was limited to relatively few terminals. For example, in the State of Hawaii, Plato terminals on the island of Oahu were available only at a single location on campus of the University of Hawaii. The only kids I ever saw using the machines were children of University staff.

In addition, Plato materials have been very difficult to transfer over to the microcomputer as that has become the predominant software vehicle in the schools. In short, the commercial costs of Plato were too high to allow its use in the schools.

The computer language BASIC was the first and, for a number of years, the only programming language available on microcomputers, other than the very inaccessible machine language. Researchers such as Tom Dwyer began in 1969 with Project Solo to investigate the possibilities of using BASIC as an interactive computing language that could be used to reform the process of teaching and learning. In an attempt to move away from the humdrum of CAI, the student was to be empowered with the ability to gain real control of the computer.

In her book[62] Solomon shows examples of computer-drawn pictures of houses obtained by clever successive applications of the PRINT statement. Dwyer and others recognized that on a certain (low) level, children could use the BASIC language to channel their curiosities and creative instincts.

Indeed, a certain computer subculture had grown up by the mid 70's created by BASIC and PC's. The difficulty with Dwyer's vision was that BASIC is after all a computer language, and as such is just not accessible to most elementary school children. Indeed, on a higher level BASIC presents a challenge to even sophisticated programmers.

Even on a more fundamental level, however, the mistake that Dwyer, Papert, and others have made in pushing programming languages in education is in expecting good results from the very availability of something having an intellectual origin or attributes.

The computer language Logo, developed by Wallace Feurzig and Seymour Papert in 1967, was a attempt to move away from the CAI software mold by creating a type of shell in which the student could learn by exploring on his own. Indeed, Papert[48] himself seemed to acknowledge the failure or at least misdirection of traditional CAI approaches to education, particularly for young children.

Logo is a computer language in the traditional AI genre, but intended for children. Indeed, it is somewhat similar to LISP, which for many years has been the dominant language of AI in placing strong emphasis on lists and placing little or no emphasis on data types. It has an added graphics feature that allows the young pupil to create geometric designs (the so-called turtle geometry) traced out by a moving object. At a certain level the programming is accessible to children, who can explore on their own in this techno-never-never land.

It seems fair to say that Logo has not rescued the computer's role as a decisive tool for education. It is, nevertheless, a more honest approach to the use of computers in the classroom, since it goes to the heart of the computer user's truest calling, namely programming. The computer is used not just as a vehicle for clever educational software, but is actually transformed into a tool in the student's hand. To use Papert's metaphor, his concept is "computer as pencil."

It must be remembered, however, that what the student is learning with Logo is **programming**, not arithmetic, not reading, not music, but **programming**. You say that the student could do a lot worse, and that may be true, but Logo fails in its honest attempt to transform the computer into an instrument of broader learning.

Logo is a natural language in which to explore notions of recursion, which are at the heart of mathematics. Certainly a bright student could be fascinated with programming simple rules of recursion and then sitting back to watch streams of interesting numerical series appear on the video screen. Can Logo teach mathematics? This question was asked and tests were performed by the Department of Artificial

Intelligence at the University of Edinburgh under the direction of James Howe. The results were mixed.

A successor to Logo, Boxer, is being developed at MIT. We seem to have come full circle and joined up with many of the same approaches of AI and, unfortunately, with the same unsolved problems encountered by that discipline.

It is interesting to note the impact, or rather lack of impact, of computers on schools espousing the Montessori philosophy[30]. From a philosophical standpoint the CAI materials clash with Montessori methods. The newer approaches embodied in the Logo language, however, are more in keeping with the independent, self-discovery Montessori methods.

Montessori schools emphasize interaction with the real environment and accordingly prepare the environment inside the classroom to achieve that goal. Therefore, programmed and audio-visual material is not as common in these schools. Although many Montessori schools have acquired computers over the past few years, the acquisitions have been fewer than average. Montessori emphasizes tactile stimuli and physical structure to convey abstract concepts. So, for example, the squares on the checkerboard are used to represent multiplication of numbers.

RECENT TRENDS

Electronic books and educational software have become multimedia productions of stereophonic sound, colorful pictures, and text. Hypertext[73] is a technique for reading and writing text while allowing the user control over how information is presented. Words can be linked to other words (also to images and sounds in "hypermedia.") Many of the CD-ROMS now being produced are hypermedia products.

This electronic recasting of children's books is not viewed favorably by all academic computer experts. David Gelernter, professor of computer science at Yale, is troubled by the fad of linking text with pictures: "To turn a book into hypertext is to invite readers to ignore exactly what counts-the story." Children are vulnerable to being seduced by the sounds and colors on a CD-ROM and may find the printed page more boring and less inviting.

It is fundamental that the development of new creative educational software is essential if the computer is to have any future role in education. But this will divert scarce resources from the teaching of fundamental skills, shoring up the ranks and salaries of capable teachers, from building maintenance, campus security, etc.

Moreover, granting for the moment that the right kind of educational software exists, that alone is not enough. A recent survey showed that there are simply not enough computer-qualified teachers available who could make use of such software in a meaningful way. Software, educational or not, is *very* labor intensive and therefore *very* costly.

What are the recent trends in educational software? There's plenty of it: last year there were more than 900 titles on the market, with new packages arriving at the rate of 150 per month, with sales around $500 million. A half-dozen heavy hitters dominate the market: The Learning Company, Microsoft, Broderbund, Davidson & Associates, Grolier, and Mindscape.

Of course, the industry has coined a new word to capture the thrust of this new educational software. It is *edutainment*. (That's Edutainment is the title of a new book and CD-ROM combination offering help through the maze of selections by Eric Brown, Osborne McGraw-Hill) To my ear that's worse than the word *infotisement*.

Some of the new titles in the genre convey the essence: *Math Blaster, the Oregon Trail, Reader Rabbit, Dinosaur Adventure*. These programs are a far cry from the simple math and reading drills that bored so many children senseless in the 1980s. They're full-scale multimedia (which just means that sound has been added) productions designed to keep children who were weaned on TV and video games interested and entertained while the author sneaks in some learning.

Likely to be among the hottest educational software coming out later this year is the Star Trek: *Omnipedia* (another horrible word!)-voice activated encyclopedia. This one will really use high-tech: the interactive electronic encyclopedia learns your voice and then responds to it. What this voice encyclopedia will do that a bound paper one cannot is beyond my comprehension.

Then there's *Explorapedia* (the names just keep getting worse!) This is Microsoft's contribution to teaching about the world of nature. From his vantage point high about Earth in the cockpit of his spacecraft, Tad leads preteens on a multimedia exploration of the world's natural environments. When a youngster clicks on one of the 15 environment types on the landscape below, the action moves down to the planet.

Once on the planet's surface, kids can click for information on any of 200 topics. Playful sound effects and music presumably enhance the experience and aid in learning. Many of the strands of Explorapedia are neither instruction nor entertainment. Cost: $34.95.

Recently, U.S. News[85] enlisted a team of children, parents, and teachers to select from over 50 off-the-shelf programs. It's evident that the selections are for entertainment as much as they are for education. In fact, I think they're intended to be downright fun. Here are three of the products they picked:

1) Edmark's Mighty Math series: Mighty Math Carnival Countdown (ages 5 to 8) leads kids through a fairgrounds where they presumably learn about logic and number sets in a bumper-car course. In Mighty Math Number Heroes (ages 8 to 11) the kids help superheroes solve problems in arithmetic, plane geometry, and probability. I suppose that the superhero powers are merely physical, since they require this kid-aid. Finally, Mighty Math Cosmic Geometry (ages 12 to 14) teaches geometry by having the

kids build on-screen robots using different geometrical shapes and can animate their creations.

2) Widget Workshop: A hands-on Science Laboratory by Maxis is an introduction to the scientific method. It provides building blocks of animal hearts, planets, and other sundries. The object is to assemble them into machines whose parts must work together according to scientific principles.
3) Weather Disaster by Discovery Communications (ages 10 and up) is very much like a slick video game. Presumably the kid learns principles of meteorology by trying to outsmart the evil Weatherman who has seized control of the atmosphere. Amid the crashes and explosions the child is expected to learn abstract principles. Yeah, right.

The price of this software? They're individually priced in the 40 to 50 dollar range: about the cost of an old-fashioned book.

CHAPTER 8

COMPUTER GAMES

Any analysis of the role of computers in education would be incomplete if it did not consider the tremendous impact that computer games have had on the youth of the country. The popularity and widespread use of these games has a great deal to do with acceptance of computers into the classroom by the children themselves. Indeed, it's often difficult to separate the games from the strictly educational software.

The video computer game market is enormous when compared to the educational software market. In 1990 annual sales of video games were already about 4 billion dollars in the United States. As a percentage of toy sales, products of the Japanese company Nintendo ran about 23% of the total as early as 1989! By 1993 Americans were spending $8.8 billion on video games. This number is predicted to grow to $14.3 billion by 1998[33].

Just to keep things in perspective, spending on educational software, although expected to grow by 30% compounded annually, will almost certainly be well below a single billion dollars by 1998. The tremendous spending on game software has likewise stimulated hardware development that in many ways surpasses what's available in the commercial PC market. The fastest Intel processor runs at about 200 million instructions per second (MIPS). Compare this to Sony's $200 "PlayStation" with a 1,000 MIPS capability. This supports much better 3-D graphics than you can get on your PC.

In his book[51] Eugene Provenzo has addressed the question: What makes computer games fun? The question is motivated by the desire to transfer the qualities at work in game software to educational software. If learning could be made as fun as Nintendo, we would really be onto something!

Many of the designers of educational software deliberately include icons and game-like features in their works familiar to the children. And all of the children know that any computer capable of running software intended to teach can just as easily run the latest games.

Provenzo cites a study by Thomas Malone, who discovered that the single most important reason for a game's popularity had to do with whether it had a specific goal. A game with a well-defined goal such as to trap a snake, shoot down alien spaceships, or to kill a monster rated highest on the "fun" scale in Malone's survey. Based on his research he argued that specific game elements be incorporated into instructional software, including

- challenge
- fantasy
- curiosity.

Interestingly enough, many of the most popular Nintendo games have these elements. In the most popular of these games the player may opt for a certain level of difficulty, i.e. design a goal that is personally meaningful. The most popular games stimulated curiosity by selectively revealing hidden information. And, of course, the subject matter and setting of the games is almost always firmly placed in fantasy worlds with exotic names: Beezo, Birdo, Ninji, Phanto, Zelda, and Link.

The view of computer games gives a glimpse into why the world of computers among school-age children is so male-dominated. According to Peter Main of Nintendo of America: "The positioning of our company has been one of total family entertainment, that we initially got to by going after boys 8 to 15, the traditional heavy users of home video. But two years later, as we examined demographics of the primary users, the biggest group of primary users continues to be boys in that 8 to 11 group..."

The subjects of the games are overwhelmingly male, and the subject matter is often downright sexist. When a female does enter, she is a "damsel in distress." Accordingly, the players themselves are male for the most part. The youth computer-game-culture is the back-room arcade and pool-room culture of but a few years ago. The girls that do appear on the scene are there to admire and support the gaming talents of their boyfriends.

One hears few complaints about either the violence or gender stereotyping that pervades video game themes. Monsters are being eaten, men are pushed off cliffs, rocket ships crash--this violence is so surrealistic that it doesn't correlate well with anything real. Consequently, the violence of video games is viewed as less threatening or damaging than, say the violence on television where real people act out simulated mayhem. The gender stereotyping and sexism may be more serious, however.

Evidently, those in the women's movement have not reviewed the cover of such popular games as *Double Dragon II, The Adventures of Bayou Billy,* or *River City Ransom.* It's enough to make even a male chauvinist pig blush. The women of the video game world are physical shells, caricatures of buxom submissive nymphs. Provenzo's book presents a thorough documentation of what he charitably terms the "amplification of gender stereotypes."

Several research surveys[48] have noted that girls participate much less than boys in the computer culture. Stanford researchers Irene Miura and Robert Hess found that three times as many boys as girls enrolled in computer camps and classes at all age levels. The proportion of girls in beginning and intermediate classes was 27 percent, a share that dropped to 14 percent in advanced programming classes, and to a vanishingly small 5 percent in higher-level courses teaching assembly language.

It has been suggested that from the beginning girls shy away from computers because they are associated with action and violence laden video games, more suited to male American cultural themes.

Recent studies on sex-linked cognitive abilities suggest that geometric intuition is keener in males than in females, whereas the situation may be reversed for linguistic ability. This is not to say that one gender is superior, it's just that the sexes use different parts of the brain. Computer games involve complex and changing geometry; it is conceivable, therefore, that they appeal more to the geometrically inclined, namely boys.

Since much of computer literacy and acumen is gained playing computer games, it is not surprising to find that males dominate and outshine the females when it comes to computers in the classroom.

My own daughter, Emilie, has openly expressed a dislike for computers. This seems unusual, since both her mother and father use computers in the home, and certainly neither have uttered a discouraging word about them. She complains about the computers in school--they are simply uninteresting to her, and only the boys excel at them. She says that none of her friends (all of who are girls) like them. All of this seems most unusual for a school whose PTA spends over half of its funds for computers and software. True to form, her older brother always had a keen interest in computers and especially in computer games like "Dungeons and Dragons."

Kids are amazingly sophisticated consumers of electronic games. The fourteen-year-old boy next door has a Sega Genesis system and Nintendo's Super NES, the dominant 16-bit platforms. He's been checking out the new game systems-- the Sony PlayStation and the Sega Saturn, not to mention the 3DO and the Atari Jaguar. Tim has definite opinions on which system performs the best and has the most realistic graphics. He knows that advertising videos of the new games coming out don't necessarily accurately reflect the real thing.

Of course, when it comes to playing the games, I am not even stand-in competition for Tim. He can beat me with his eyes closed. It's a generation thing.

CHAPTER 9

THE ELECTRONIC CLASSROOM

Equipped with video conferencing abilities, electronic notetaking and visual class participation programs, the electronic classroom enables students to interact with fellow students and professors more than in the traditional classroom and transforms students into more active learners. Or, is it that computers are replacing teachers and creating button-pushing mutes of students who, for the most part, are passively reacting to the flickering screen?

Before computers, television was the last major technology to be disseminated en masse. Just forty years ago, it held the promise of educating the young and bringing culture to remote areas. Today, commercial television programming is viewed by many as a vast wasteland. There are few remaining who continue to view television of whatever genre as having a central role in the education of children. It could be argued that television has at least fulfilled its promise of disseminating culture. Many, however, would quarrel with the virtues of that accomplishment.

The first application of electronic gadgetry to the classroom appeared in the form of televised teaching, i.e. the practice of remote teaching via a video link to one or usually several classroom sites. This doesn't strictly fall into the category of computer usage in the classroom, but nevertheless is relevant to the subject, since students are constrained to watch a video monitor.

Most educators have acknowledged the value of being able to bring expert teaching to a remote area that would otherwise be denied. However, everyone would agree that the equipment involved, i.e., the video screen, loudspeakers, etc., is at best neutral to the learning process. Put another way, learning is in no way enhanced by the televideo process itself.

Robert D. Putnam is a Harvard Professor who has documented a sharp decline in the percentage of people in this country joining groups of any kind, be they political, choral, fraternal, church, or hobby. His essay, "Bowling Alone" captured national attention in focusing on the impact of the introduction of television in the 1950s and its influence on the decline in both social trust and group participation. If social isolation and decline of trust is to be blamed in part on television, can the influence of computers on these factors be far different?

EDUCOM is a 29 year-old consortium of nearly 600 colleges and universities and 122 companies involved in computing. EDUCOM has played a leading role in encouraging the use of technology in higher education. Officials set forth a plan[15], the "National Learning Infrastructure Initiative," at the organization's annual meeting to demonstrate how technology might be used to improve instruction and cut costs in higher education.

The Clinton Administration had also made such a proposal. According to Carol A. Twigg, a vice-president of EDUCOM, the effort would try to link many of the small projects related to distance learning and to classroom instruction already underway. EDUCOM officials rejected suggestions that the involvement of high-tech companies would make some people skeptical of the whole effort. "We're not looking to sell machines," said Ms. Twigg. "The focus in this case is really on the creation of learning tools."

More than 3,000 people were expected to attend the November meeting of EDUCOM in San Antonio[71]. Several lawmakers have made use of EDUCOM as a reliable resource when wrestling with issues concerning the proposed National Information Infrastructure.

Recently several projects within EDUCOM were killed including Project EASI (equal access to software and information), which helps people with disabilities, an annual awards program recognizing innovation in software intended for use in higher education, and a project to set forth a list of rights and responsibilities for educators in the electronic environment. There appears to be more than a little dissension within EDUCOM with regard to which projects should receive emphasis and which should be terminated.

Mr. Robert C. Heterick, Jr., says EDUCOM has spent much of the past year laying the groundwork for what it calls its "Grand Challenges" project. The group hopes to demonstrate what it sees as the need for information technology in higher education. He expects technology to foster a more learner-centered environment and to have an impact on the teaching and learning process. An additional payoff is that, according to Heterick, technology does something about the cost issues and about the access-to-higher-education issues.

An infotisement of Apple Computer Inc. proclaims: "Faculty at Penn State Computerize Huge Agricultural Course." Dr. Harold Harpster, Professor of animal science, declares: "There is no doubt that our students prefer the Macintosh computer over other computing platforms." The University has expanded multimedia-based teaching by equipping classrooms with state-of-the-art technologies, including computers, laser disc players, VCRs, and fiber-optic connections. For example, instructors can take pictures in the field and present them during the next class period. "We can photograph something happening in our laboratories or on our farms and actually present it in class minutes later," Dr. Harpster says.

And then there's the technology designed to relieve the student of the "burden" of note taking. The title of a recent article "Pen-Based Computer Seen as Tool to Ease Burden of Note Taking[32]" pretty much sums up its contents. A professor's electronic "whiteboard" on the classroom wall is connected to students' pen-based computers, so that the students could receive notes directly, without having to copy information from the board.

According to a spokesperson for the technology, Dave Berque, a professor of computer science at Depauw University, "The system is not designed to replace traditional note taking, but enhance it." He disputes any suggestion that his system could lead to glassy-eyed students watching passively as class notes simply appear before them. "Instructors," he says, "will have to choose carefully the material they write on the electronic board." Mr. Berque says he realizes his system will never completely replace traditional blackboards, since copying what a professor is writing is often part of the learning process.

One is left to wonder in what manner Mr. Berque's system could supplement traditional notetaking. Why not just buy one of the many professionally taken "crib-notes" on the market at the student bookstore? They would cost thousands less than the pen-based computers and be less distracting to boot.

The Networked Classroom

Increasingly, the electronic classroom is synonymous with the networked classroom. These are classrooms with several PCs connected to a local area network (LAN) and also connected to a wide area network (WAN). The students can send messages to one or more of their friends, or perhaps to the entire class. They also can access the Internet or one of the on-line services.

The Clinton administration has proposed to give every school and library in the United States free basic access to the Internet[43]. The cost for wiring the nations 100,000 public grade schools and 9,000 libraries as well as private, nonprofit schools with endowments of less than $50 million would be covered by the communications carriers themselves. And, of course, they would pass these costs on to their paying customers. Republicans are claiming that the Democrats caved-in to the interests of the teacher unions, who, they say, want to avoid any real education reform. It is interesting that throwing money at the schools for technology has become so politicized.

It will not be many years before access to the Internet will mean effective and timely access to information valuable to school children. At this point it's difficult to predict how much an improvement this will be over traditional avenues of information. One thing is for sure, however, it will be hard to beat a good encyclopedia set in the foreseeable future. The virtues of schools being wired for purposes of two-way communication are far less evident.

More than two decades ago a two-way radio link was initiated between the University of Hawaii and students in American Samoa. The link proved to be immensely popular with the students who chatted endlessly. Topics of conversation were largely limited to trivial matters: the weather, sports, pass-time pursuits, etc. It's safe to say, however, that there was little or no educational payoff or even cultural exchange from this communication link.

Designers of the networked classroom are expecting much the same thing that the planners of the Hawaii-Samoa radio link expected. They reason that the mere fact of being networked will bring knowledge to those who are linked or wired. It didn't happen two decades ago in Hawaii, and I don't see it happening in classrooms today.

Advocates for networking are following a model for how the human brain works. A "neural network" is a collection of interconnected "nodes," each node having one or several inputs and outputs. In the brain the nodes are the neuron cells.

For more than twenty years engineers have built hardware and software circuits based on the neural net model. These circuits are capable of adapting to input and have found a number of engineering applications. Neural nets can be "trained" to recognize certain inputs and have therefore taken a central role in the latest AI research.

Interestingly enough, a recent theoretical result demonstrates that a computer based on neural nets is really more powerful than the classical "Turing Machine" model of the computer. The neural net machine has capabilities beyond that of the procedural computer.

While it may be the case that the network paradigm has theoretical capabilities beyond that of a procedural system, it doesn't follow that this architecture by itself creates knowledge or even encourages the dissemination of information among its nodes. Besides, we already have in place elaborate systems for the exchange of information at long range. That's what the facsimile machine and the telephones are for.

The Computer Room

The common practice of schools and universities is to reserve a special room containing computers set aside for students to use, the famous "computer room." A strong association is thereby formed between "the room" and using the computer. The deleterious effect is that the computer is not integrated with other studies and activities. When away from the room, there is no thought given to it.

If the intent is to teach students basic skills using the computer, then the computer-as-teacher idea is doomed right out of the starting gate. On the other hand if that is not their intent, then students have any business in the computer room in the first place.

The idea of a computer room has proven such an abject failure that most administrators have had to toss it out. Consequently, the recent push has been to disperse the computers into the school classrooms and into the dorm rooms at the university in an attempt to integrate them into other activities.

The difficulty with the latter approach is that at many schools such as my daughter's, even though there is no longer a computer room, the computer is only used when a special teacher trained in teaching the subject comes to the classroom. The effect is the same as if there were an isolated room set aside, only now it's an isolated time. When the computer teacher is not there, the row of one-eyed silent dumb terminals stares back at the class.

CHAPTER 10

COMPUTERS IN THE CLASSROOM: BIG BUSINESS

Instructional Technology businesses will rake in some $4 billion[85] this year from elementary, middle and high schools, twice as much as five years ago. President Clinton has proposed an additional $2 billion in federal money so that "every 12-year-old can log on to the Internet." Well-meaning parents and parent-teacher organizations pour additional millions of dollars into computer hardware and software. A million here, a billion there; computerization of the classroom could add up to some real money, most of which is not a one-time cost.

The Clinton administration has been at the forefront of activity to computerize classrooms across America. In March, the President joined 20,000 volunteers and 2,000 businesses in California as they installed about 6 million feet of wire to connect 2,600 schools to the Internet. What will it cost to implement the administration's proposal to wire all US schools and libraries for the Internet? No one really knows exactly. However, the Commerce Department estimated[43] it would require $1.5 billion annually to provide schools with the most basic telephone-line Internet connection. This figure does not include monthly Internet access charges, cost of the computers, or teacher training.

These expenditures on high tech just don't make sense when one takes a look at the condition of the buildings and facilities of the nation's schools. They are a national disgrace. It is estimated that about

14 million US children attend schools so decrepit and in need of repair that they are a threat to health and an impediment to education[78]. Leaking roofs, exposed asbestos, dirty walls, and non-functioning heaters and air conditioners plague schools, not only in West Virginia, but also in Missouri and even in the golden State of California. Unfortunately, wiring the kids to the Internet has a much better chance of getting funded than making badly needed repairs to their schools.

At present there are approximately 9 children for every computer in US schools. A recent study by the Department of Education concluded that the ratio should be closer to 5 to one. Currently only 4 percent of classrooms meet that requirement. A recent study by McKinsey & Co., a management firm, estimates the total 10-year cost of meeting this and other technology goals at $109 billion! Clearly, there's a lot of money to be made in classroom technology.

U.S. Secretary of Education Richard W. Riley has been an outspoken advocate of computers in the classroom. "Computers are the 'new basic' of American education, and the Internet is the blackboard of the future," Riley said, "but the future is here and now, and we cannot miss this opportunity to help all of our young people grow and thrive. I strongly believe that if we help all of our children learn the basics and become technologically literate, we will give a generation of young people the skills they need to enter this new knowledge and information driven economy[86]."

Riley sees the federal government acting in cooperation with local governments and the private sector to promote massive infusion of computer technology into the classroom. "Although the federal government has an important role in helping to galvanize efforts," Riley said, "the challenge is a clarion call to local communities and states and to the private and non-profit sectors from which leadership and initiative must come." The plan was to match federal dollars and in kind contributions from state, local, and private sources.

Computer companies and their affiliates have been only too willing to answer the clarion call. Groundwork in the form of computer donations for corporate write-offs and strategy planning was laid early in Clinton's first term.

The rush was on. IBM donated hundreds of PCs to schools and libraries[87]. The magazine Computerworld launched a multi-pronged plan to put millions of computers in US classrooms[88]. The magazine's publisher Gary Beach called on Congress to pass legislation that would encourage US corporations to donate computers to American schools. He proposed that they get a tax credit ($100) for fully depreciated machines. Beach said there is approximately 50 million PC's in American corporations of which approximately 40% are fully depreciated. "The Computers for Classrooms Project," said Beach, "will put badly needed technology in our classrooms. We have to act now to make certain students excel."

As part of its campaign strategy Computerworld began to court academics with connection to computer education. At the Fourth annual Computerworld Smithsonian Awards dinner Dr. Ronald Thornton, of Tufts University was honored for his development of information technology tools that have "helped thousands of students grasp scientific concepts that traditionally are hard to understand."

Apples for the Classroom

Apple Computers pioneered the personal computer assault on the classrooms of America. To most manufacturers, the school and college markets are primarily "door-openers" for building sales of personal computers. The home and commercial markets are much larger. Thus, Apple, for example, provided ten thousand Apple II's to schools in California, and it promised a computer to almost every school in the nation if a tax proposal to grant tax breaks for such donations were to pass. (Such a proposal introduced by California Congressman Fortney Stark (D-Contra Costa County) failed to be enacted.)

Apple's executives had more than the educational benefit of school children in mind when they demonstrated their largesse. They knew full well that if the parents of just a few of the students in every Apple classroom were to buy an Apple of their own, the company would ring up big profits. This was a conscious well-thought-out marketing strategy[58].

Intended as a follow-up to the Apple II, the Apple IIGS was launched in October 1986 with superb color graphics and stereo sound capabilities. Executives at Apple acknowledged the less than satisfactory classroom performance of the old Apple IIs. In his book John Scully writes:

> "The personal computer's promise has been far from fulfilled. Most of the computers on school desks today are used for simple drills and rote learning. We're still preparing our children for the same old repetitive jobs in the industrial age-the very jobs that are disappearing daily. Instead, we should be preparing them for the jobs of the future, jobs that will require thinking skills, not rote memorization and repetition."

SAFEWAY CASH REGISTER TAPES FOR CLASSROOM COMPUTERS

In an effort to get in on the computer boom in 1994 Safeway Stores instituted a program to encourage its customers to save their register receipts. Receipts totaling so many thousand dollars are then redeemed for computers for the local school. What a clever marketing idea! Safeway gets more business and good will in the community to boot.

Safeway's program says worlds about how computers for education are viewed by the public, namely, a holy quest worthy of sacrifice. Could you imagine the following program: "Safeway Register Tapes for making repairs to the local elementary school?" I can't.

The new approach intended to rescue the computer as a teaching tool was, and remains to the present day, the multimedia approach. "The personal computer provides us with a better 'book,' one which is active (like the child) rather than passive. Future generations of the personal computer will offer the attention-grabbing powers of TV, but be controllable by the child rather than the networks."

The operative phrase here is "attention-grabbing powers." Somehow we, the objects of Scully's marketing blandishments, are to believe that the addition of color to the graphics and stereo sound will transform the dull ineffective machine into a thing of wonder and enlightenment-to borrow a phrase from Apple's marketing prose: the personal computer will become a "bicycle for the mind."

The old educational software company founded by Suppes in 1967, Computer Curriculum Corp., is the fastest-growing unit of Simon & Schuster, and Simon & Schuster is the world's largest educational publisher. CCC develops and markets software for K-12 schools. The company's SuccessMaker product is instructional software that integrates reading, math and science modules to create, according to company advertising, an individualized learning experience for each student. The company claims that its "intelligent tutoring" is based on 25 years of educational research and has proven itself in increased student performance throughout the 7,500 schools currently using SuccessMaker.

CCC has just designated Woodlawn Elementary in Danville, Kentucky, a model school site because of the decision of the school officials to install a 27-station computer network running SuccessMaker in the Fall of 1995.

PRIVATIZATION OF PUBLIC SCHOOLS

Education Alternatives Inc.[76g] recently took charge of nine ailing Baltimore schools. Most of these schools were in blighted neighborhoods and reflected the poverty and low achievement levels of the surrounding community. Educators and community leaders had hopelessly run out of ideas to extricate the children attending these schools from tracks leading to disaster.

Now that Education Alternatives has taken over, school grounds have never been cleaner, student attendance is better, parents are more involved, and classrooms are stocked with computers that students use every day. Every classroom has at least four computers, and every school has several computer labs. In all, Education Alternatives has installed a whopping 1,400 computers, since the contract started three years ago. Are standardized test scores, which measure student performance, any higher? No, hardly any at all.

What is happening in the Baltimore Public School system is happening at many other urban school systems around the country. When test scores do improve, it's because greater emphasis is given to teaching basic reading and writing skills. The computers are window dressing. They may make the parents feel proud; it's a sure fire way for the private company running the school to please, and little or no ingenuity is required to order up a thousand or so PCs or Macs.

The several million dollars that is spent to purchase, install, and run the computers is a significant portion of the $135 million dollar five-year contract. But the bad news is that it's an expenditure has very little real payoff.

School officials are understandably wary of Education Alternatives' aims, especially in view of the stagnant test scores. Some have complained that the company is using the system as a marketing tool in order to gain lucrative contracts elsewhere. Kurt L. Schmoke, Mayor of Baltimore, has stated that he wants to negotiate a new contract with Education Alternatives that includes student performance goals.

CHAPTER 11

ACADEMICIANS' VIEWS OF COMPUTERS IN THE CLASSROOM

Academicians' views are divergent on the subject of the value of computers in education. Mathematicians, however, are probably the most skeptical of any group. Some have suggested that this is because computers represent a threat to mathematics as an occupation, as if mathematicians sat around all day doing what computers do, only more slowly.

Do theoretical mathematicians really fear computers as a threat to their occupation? Many of those who have embraced computers think so, and they aren't all ignorant bumpkins. Expressing such a view, an associate professor of marketing at the University of Wisconsin recently wrote[12]:

> *"...The real myth, of course is that theoretical mathematics is useful in the computer age. Calculus and other theoretical-math courses should be replaced with computer programming and computer-simulation courses whenever possible.*
>
> *Theoretical mathematicians are teaching the "latest" in ox-cart technology in the age of the jet airplane. They are the "blacksmiths" of the computer age.*
>
> *No one group fears computers more than theoretical mathematicians. They see them as ending their way of life (and the sooner the better, for the sake of our undergraduate and graduate students).*

Few individuals with any knowledge at all of the history of science would agree with the ridiculous view that theoretical mathematics has no use. There really is no need to rebut such a statement. The mere fact, however, that someone associated with education, even if not science education, would express such an opinion raises a red flag.

The people who know mathematics best and have given thought to the role of technology in the classroom are very aware of the damage to real learning that has been wrought by its misuse. These are the mathematics professors at major institutions around the country. In a recent editorial comment in the American Mathematical Monthly[23] John Duncan, a professor of mathematics at the University of Arkansas, writes:

> *"Some of us who were very early to use technology to alleviate drudgery, to visualize graphs and surfaces, to conduct helpful numerical experiments, etc., are now alarmed at its use as a substitute for thinking. It even seems to deter problem-solvers from producing general mathematical proofs by holding their focus to computing a few numerical examples."*

The thinking behind this is well understood among university mathematicians, and few among this group would fail to agree with Duncan's comment. Unfortunately, university professors of both pure and applied math have almost nothing to say about the teaching of mathematics in elementary and secondary schools and surprisingly little to say even about how and what mathematics is taught at their own institutions. Many parts of the latter domain have been inherited and left almost unchanged over the eons, or, whatever changes and additions to the curriculum that have been made, have been largely left to those specializing in "math ed."

Academic mathematicians, for whatever reason, have not made their influence felt among the masses in the same way that, say, academic physicists or astronomers have. The overall numbers probably explain why mathematicians' influence is so small. One simple reason is that there are so few. Since 1986 there have been on-average less than one thousand doctorates awarded annually by American Universities in the mathematical sciences (pure mathematics, statistics, applied mathematics, and operations research). Of these one thousand fully a half are non-US citizens, many of whom return to their homes abroad after completing their studies[83].

There are fewer Ph.D. mathematicians in the US than there are attorneys in the city of Washington D.C.! Despite their small number the nation is unable to absorb the few new math Ph.D.s coined each year. A 1991 survey by the American Mathematical Society and the Mathematics Association of America reported an alarming 12 percent of the 1990-91 doctorates were unemployed and seeking employment in November 1991; by the spring of 1992 this number had fallen to 5 percent-still a very high number for what one might think is an elite highly employable group.

The reasons for the failure of mathematics to attract a popular following may lie with the nature of the subject. Mathematical reasoning does not lend itself to popularization in the way most other subjects do. Even theoretical physics can be made "real" by Feynman diagrams or photos of the Stanford linear accelerator. How does one depict, for example, the concepts of Lie Group and Modular function that led to the proof of Fermat's conjecture? Mathematics, the Queen of the Sciences, may in fact be a poor peasant outside of the inner circle. There are no mathematical equivalents of Carl Sagan or Richard Feynman.

The best known of the writers of popular mathematics is probably Martin Gardner, but his best known material consists of collections of puzzles. Whenever a mathematical accomplishment does make it to the public light, it is almost always treated as the result of puzzle solving rather than as an activity associated with an active body of knowledge.

The recent well-publicized proof of Fermat's Last Theorem by Andrew Wiles made no use of computer technology.

This happens to be another unfortunate example of mathematical research misunderstood not only by the public at large, but even by those who would write a popular book on the subject.

Marilyn vos Savant's recent book, *The World's Most Famous Math Problem*[54], is a case in point. Nigel Boston and Andrew Granville[6] wrote a technically accurate review of this book. The bottom line is that vos Savant is way out of her water and doesn't even begin to understand Wiles' work. Among all the sciences, mathematics alone seems destined to bear such a tragic cross!

Wiles' proof of the Fermat Theorem is fashioned from a lattice of very deep and modern concepts, all of which stand apart from computer technology. The proof reveals the truth of the fact that no triple of positive whole numbers a, b, and c can ever satisfy a relation of the type

$$a^n + b^n = c^n$$

for n a whole number equal to 3 or greater.

A computer could be used to seek (now we know without success) various relations of this sort, but such a search, which must necessarily eventually end, could never by itself establish the truth of what Fermat guessed at three hundred years ago.

One could justifiably argue that Fermat's Theorem has no practical value, although it would be difficult to deny its interest and beauty. It would be folly, however, to conclude that the proof's techniques employed and developed over many decades will never find applicability elsewhere.

Although few research mathematicians would disagree with John Duncan's view, it would be a mistake, however, to convey the impression that all university professors are of one mind on the subject of computers and calculators in mathematics education.

For almost two decades, Ohio State University mathematics professors Bert Waits and Frank Demana have been using hand-held calculators to prepare future freshmen for the rigors of calculus. They made calculators part of a remedial program called "Calculator and Computer Precalculus Project," also known as C^2PC, to create a new approach to high-school mathematics. They claim that teachers began to have "fun," and doing mathematics became talked about and seen in an entirely new light.

Waits estimates that more than fifty thousand students have been through the program. Although the C^2PC's results haven't been formally or objectively evaluated, Waits claims, "We have a lot of informal evidence to suggest that, in the long run, we're doing these kids a lot of good. ...Do C^2PC students do better on traditional paper-and-pencil-exams? We really don't care. Exactness is overemphasized in school mathematics.[75]"

The statement that exactness is overemphasized in the schools is troubling enough. I don't believe that Waits was referring to making numerical estimations in favor of exactness, since calculators aren't really useful for that. Leaving this aside, it is my belief that experiences such as those encountered by Waits and Demana do not contradict the conclusion that for the majority of students hand-held calculators are essentially of no use for learning of basic skills. One clue to this is Waits' and Demana's own statements that they have no hard evidence of improvement of students' skills on paper and-pencil-exams.

What other kinds of exams are there? Presumably their students' performance on exams focused on hand-held calculators has improved. The students have learned the correct sequence of buttons on the calculator to push in order to achieve a desired result. Does this mean that they have learned any mathematics? I don't think so.

The students targeted by Waits and Demana required remedial mathematics, even though many had endured four full years of high-school mathematics. In short, these students were floundering and turned off by the system. The hand-held calculators with their ability to produce graphs, etc. gave these students a "fun" respite. Any real learning of mathematics took place incidental to their use. The "fun" enjoyed was not obtained without high monetary cost, money that could have been better spent on teacher training, improving teacher salaries, and hiring more teachers.

The author and mathematician John A. Paulos has emphasized the need for learning how to make intelligent numerical estimations. Shoppers often need to make quick decisions based on cost estimates. A good engineer probably makes more decisions based on estimates than he does based on exact calculations, although the latter may certainly be required to build the final product.

Are computers or calculators helpful in making numerical estimations? I don’t see how. The central ingredient involved in making estimation does not require arithmetic operations; it requires intuition about numbers.

Balance is required in effectively integrating calculators and computers into both the schools and the workplace. These instruments have their place, but usually they should not be instruments of first resort. A good engineer doesn't just whip out his calculator; first he reflects; perhaps then with pencil makes a "back of the envelope" calculation. Then later he will run exact numbers on his calculator or computer to verify what his intuition has told him.

If calculators and computers are to be effectively used in teaching they should likewise be employed in a balanced manner. This generally means that the instruments are on the back end of the process. They may reinforce intuition and provide a confirmation of principles that have been learned, but they cannot engender intuition or substitute for learning.

CHAPTER 12

COMPUTERS IN ACADEMIA

If universities across the nation have not been the cradle of the computer revolution, they have quickly become its focus and ideological center. If you want to hear the clarion call of the computer revolution, don't listen to the politicians, or the lobbyists, but to the university administrators. Richard Cyert, president of Carnegie-Mellon, a traditional leader in computer technology, announced over ten years ago that "The great University of the Future will be that with a great computer system[70]."

Donald Langenberg, chancellor of the University of Maryland system sees the electronic networks and digitized data banks as an epochal change, "the first change in the underlying technology of knowledge in 500 years[76d]." He believes that the university will be completely transformed; the basic elements will change, "the most basic units of what faculty members do-the course, the credit unit, the semester, the library, the campus."

What Langenberg is saying is that students don't need to be in a classroom; they can obtain instruction on-line. And what about the professor? When asked about the scarcity of Aristotle-quality professors, he replied, "Oh, but that's the beauty of it. You can get wonderful packages. With the best economist in the world on 3-D CD-ROM, full color, in your living room, should you really get in your car and go sit in a classroom at the local community college and hear a less brilliant professor *quoting* the world's best economists?"

These pronouncements mistake "professor-in-a-can" for a real-live professor. Human nature and the needs of learning require inspiration and interaction with a real-live professor, even if he has not won a Noble prize, and even if his lecture style leaves something to be desired. Technology may send an image and voice hundreds of miles away to reach a wider audience, but it should not eliminate the teacher even if there are "books" capable of talking.

Campus Networks

An examination of the actual uses of campus computer networks reveals that a great deal of it has questionable educational content. Recently, Carnegie Mellon announced[56] that it would eliminate from its computer network the set of Internet discussion groups devoted to sex. To say the least, the focus and interest of these groups is not academic. On-line civil liberties activists say the university's action has broad implications. "It's like banning Henry Miller from the library," said Mike Godwin, staff counsel for the Electronic Frontier Foundation, the Washington based civil liberties and policy group. "This is a pure academic freedom issue."

The sexually oriented "news groups" are among the most popular on the Usenet. Some of the sexually oriented groups are devoted to hard-core photographs that users can display on their computers. Some groups feature only text.

Bill Arm, CMU's vice president for computer services decided CMU should consider restricting access to the sexually oriented newsgroups after reading Pennsylvania's obscenity laws and cruising the Internet[56]. Once he saw what was on the network, he feared that the school could be held liable as a purveyor of pornography. "We really do believe in free speech, and we work very hard not to cut it back," Arm said. "But the law of the land says there are limits to what is protected by the First Amendment." This same problem has come up at a number of universities: Iowa State University, Penn State University, and Stanford to name three.

A few short days later the Carnegie Mellon ban of all sexually oriented on-line discussion groups from the campus computer network was largely rescinded, apparently under pressure from the civil liberties community, which compared the restriction to banning books from the school library. An e-mail announcement by the president of CMU's student body, Declan B. McCullagh, indicated that students and administrators agreed to ... "create a standing committee made up of faculty, staff, and students to decide what news groups to remove or reinstate. University officials removed the news groups containing sexually explicit pictures the day before, but the new committee will review decision. The text news groups will be allowed to continue on-line."

Many colleges are requiring computer purchase by incoming freshmen. The idea is controversial, sometimes resulting in protests by students, such as by the recent group of Wake Forest University students[21]. There the computer requirement is part of a series of changes in the curriculum that will increase the annual tuition by $3,000 for freshmen who enter that year. Supporters of the mandatory computer purchase plan say that folding the cost of a machine into tuition insures that all students have them-not just those whose families can afford them.

In pushing for the mandatory computers some administrators have been accused of laying the groundwork for greater use of distance learning. In general, however, the opposition to the tidal wave of PC's is token and seems doomed to failure. There is simply too much impetus behind it: administrators who find a lot of support among parents, and the computer suppliers themselves, good business people that they are, who would put a PC under every toadstool if given the opportunity. In many ways it's surprising and ironic that these bastions of academic talent and pure thought should succumb so easily to the blandishments of a commercial industry.

COMPUTERS IN LAW SCHOOL

At the Harvard Law School the required "Introduction to Lawyering" course for fall 1994 has focused exclusively on the Simpson murder trial[14]. The course, which the professor, Charles Nesson, has subtitled "CyberLaw" relies on computers for both research and writing. This sets the course apart from more traditional approaches to legal instruction. According to Nesson, the future of legal research rests with e-mail, Internet, Lexis, Nexis and other electronic media. He feels that this course provides the opportunity to introduce students to computer resources.

Nesson acknowledged some start-up difficulties. "The whole enterprise was directed toward getting the first year students into an electronic environment. This is the first class we have given e-mail addresses to. Some were familiar with it; some weren't. This has caused big problems." Nesson indicated that he has his own concerns about the course. "The biggest problem is keeping it clear that what we're about is educating students," he said. "The lure of publicity can be corrupting."

At a number of law schools, including George Mason in Fairfax, Virginia, students are given personal accounts gratis with access to LEXIS and NEXIS as well as WestLaw. These are costly on-line services that are ordinarily available to only the most affluent students, or indeed the most affluent legal firms. These enterprises are counting on the next generation of lawyers becoming dependent upon the sources of on-line information they provide.

Attending the right graduate school and being published in prestigious journals are still important, but apparently in some circles establishing a name for oneself on line has become the newest way to win recognition[19]. Indeed, if one becomes a known entity on the network by regular communication with academic pals in Greece, New Zealand and elsewhere, a case can be made that one has achieved international significance, one of the touchstones in going for academic promotion or tenure.

This drive to become known in an electromagnetic medium is reminiscent of the days when citizen band (CB) radios were popular, especially down on the interstate. One's personality and purpose in life was then defined by maintenance of a network of contacts with similar minded people. The "handles" often gave a clue as to the individual's personality or profession: Sad Sally, Minnie the Moocher, and Salesman Sam. All achieved recognition, respect, and a measure of local, if not international, significance.

Access to Internet mailing lists has touched off a firestorm of controversy at various Universities[16]. Exchanging electronic mail on a list, some say, falls somewhere between participating in a telephone conference call and publishing an article in a journal. According to one side of the argument the lists are forums for informal, frank discussion among colleagues and not for the public at large. Others argue that a public institution cannot allow its faculty to maintain private domains. The freedom-of-information and open-meeting laws, they say, will require them to release mailing-list messages exchanged on their computers. I believe it was Henry Kissinger who said that squabbles between academics are so fierce precisely because the rewards to the victor are so small.

In September 1994 at the Commerce Department the Clinton administration hosted[20] a meeting of about 100 users and producers of copyrighted materials to begin looking into questions on how the electronic age impacts copyright matters. Attendees included educators, attorneys, motion picture industry people, and publishers. The principle topic for exploration was how the "fair use" provision of the Copyright Act transfers to electronic materials.

The "fair use" provision allows educators, librarians, researchers, and journalists to use protected materials in limited ways without having to compensate owners of the copyrights. Copyright owners are reluctant to extend such rights because they fear the number of copies of electronic documents will dilute the copyright values.

Issues relating to copyright laws have slowed the spread of the multi-media hypertext technique as users and owners of copyrights scramble to redefine and interpret the protection afforded by the laws on the books.

Many similar questions have arisen in the academic world. For example, developers of educational software are uncertain if copyrighted material could be included in their programs. Those offering long-distance courses were uncertain whether they could distribute copyrighted materials over airways and computer networks. Future meetings of subgroups from the initial convocation are scheduled for the coming months.

A group of scholars is attempting to establish a university entirely on the Internet[36]. Part-time instructors would be paid \$125 for each student; tuition would be \$200 per course. Financial support for the Virtual Online University is uncertain, but the conferencing software known as MOO ("multi-user dimension, object-oriented") is available. By activating various computerized "objects," students and teachers could meet in classrooms, break into small seminars, and visit various campus buildings.

Organizers of Virtual Online University hope it will be the first of its kind to be recognized by an accrediting agency. The organizers predict multitudinous benefits. For example, students who are normally silent in traditional classes could become active participants in the new university. Certainly a whole new approach would have to be thought out by professors, encouraging them to move toward a "transdisciplinary" approach.

ELECTRONIC SCHOLARLY JOURNALS

Traditional printed journals have been the mainstay of scholarly work for hundreds of years. For many fields, including mathematics, their days are now numbered. Two factors are driving the impending changes. The first is the growth in the size of the scholarly literature; the second is the growth in electronic media storage capabilities coupled with the diminution of associated costs.

Good mathematics libraries spend over $100,000 annually just on journal subscription costs and least another $200,000 on space to store them and staff to manage them. Altogether the approximately fifty thousand mathematical papers published each year would require about 2.5 gigabytes of storage. A 7-gigabyte capacity disk now costs between two and three hundred dollars-less than the cost of a single journal subscription!

In view of these numbers, it just doesn't make any sense to maintain a paper journal archive. The paper journals, however, will not disappear over night; there will be some lag in converting old paper journals over to the electronic format. A new set of standards will have to be developed together with software to search and download articles bearing on a specific topic or by a particular individual. But much of that already exists anyway.

There will certainly be a period of painful adjustment, not a little having to do with the psychological impact of no longer being able to see one's cherished work appear in the familiar paper journal proudly lying in full view of the world in hundreds of libraries around the world. Paper copies of a scholarly work will be for temporary use only by those who have specific interests in the subject.

The benefits of the changeover to electronic archiving of scholarly journals justify the interim pain. Not only will costs come down, but also the publication process itself will be facilitated greatly. Backlogs and delays will disappear.

CHAPTER 13

COMPUTERS FOR RESEARCH

As number cruncher the modern computer has proved to be a boon to all of the applied sciences, physical and social. The operative word here is "applied." Searching large databases of chemical compounds or databases of population distributions for desired characteristics would not otherwise have been possible. However, to know what to look for, to know what to theorize, that is a different story. To look for instances where theory is advanced by computers, a reasonable test would be to consider the case of mathematics, since after all computers would *seem* to be most closely related to that subject.

Is the computer a relevant investigative tool for research in pure mathematics? The famous mathematician Carl Frederick Gauss (1777-1855) conjectured the celebrated Prime Number Theorem by studying tables of prime numbers. Prime numbers are the basic building blocks of all the whole numbers.

A prime number is by definition a whole number only divisible by itself and the number one. The number "one' itself is excluded from the list of primes. So the list begins: 2, 3, 5, 7, 11, 13, 17, 19, etc. The famous Greek geometer, Euclid, gave a proof that this list of primes does not terminate and is, therefore, an infinite list.

The Prime Number Theorem tells with what density the prime numbers are distributed among all of the natural (counting) numbers, and Gauss was able to guess (although others provided the proof much later) the correct distribution of the primes by pouring over tables.

Had he the opportunity, he might have scanned computer screens of even larger tables of primes. It is significant that Gauss made his conjecture without a computer, and even more significant that a computer would have provided no additional clues to arrive at a proof of the conjecture.

An article that recently appeared in the Scientific American[35] proclaimed the "Death of Proof." The author suggested that classical proofs within a conceptual framework were to be replaced by visualization and verification on a computer. The computer would account for all difficult considerations as, for example, in Andrew Wiles' recent proof of Fermat's Last Theorem. Indeed, Wiles' proof was characterized as a "splendid anachronism." The article released a flood of indignant protests, even from mathematicians quoted in the article.

That such an article could appear in a venerable and respectable publication points up the extent to which both the computer's capabilities and mathematicians' works are so profoundly misunderstood. The computer was of no value (that's zero!) in this triumphal conquest.

The computer does not correct for intellectual myopia in the way eyeglasses correct for visual myopia, nor is it a Hubble telescope for the mind. The computer does not enhance our intelligence in the way an electronic hearing aid enhances our perception of sound. What the computer does is to do things that we already understand how to do, and do them much faster. It may check a thousand or even many thousand cases of an equation in the time it takes a human to verify only one. In carrying out these operations with such speed the computer may *seem* to be omniscient, it may even *seem* to be thinking, but it cannot and does not.

There are some mathematicians today who use the computer to arrive at conjectures about numbers by examining a large number of cases or instances of numerical expressions. These searches almost never suggest a course of proof or verification of the conjecture. The fact that the Riemann hypothesis (perhaps the most famous of all conjectures in mathematics) has been verified to some astronomically large value by computers does not bring the proof one iota closer to realization. Neither does it add any additional intuition nor suggest approaches to take in formulating a proof.

Such calculations pretty much do exactly what they claim to do: verify the conjecture out to a certain point. Therefore, at least one would know to search for counterexamples to the hypothesis beyond the point the computer left off.

Frequently, mathematical calculations of this sort serve to "benchmark" a particular computer's capability, or more often provide friendly sports competition among competing groups of computer scientists. Which group now holds the record to the number of places of "pi" (the ratio of the circumference to the diameter of a circle) calculated? Or for the largest Merscene prime calculated?

One might mention the famous solution to the Four Color Theorem accomplished in 1976 by Kenneth Appel and Wolfgang Hacken of the University of Illinois as running counter to the claim that computers have not been used to provide mathematical intuition. The Four-Color Theorem states that any conceivable flat map of the countries of the world can always be colored using four (or fewer) distinct colors while maintaining the requirement that adjacent countries are assigned different colors.

This well-known result is often cited as the first such relying upon the use of computers for its proof. One estimate was that it would take a human working 60 hour weeks about 100,000 years to check the same cases that the computer checked to complete the proof[24].

The Four-Color Problem is a rare occurrence of the decisive intervention of the computer in a pure mathematical research endeavor. The computer has seldom played any role whatsoever in mathematical research, and where it has played a role, it has generally been a very minor one.

The framework for the proof and the conception of the proof of the Four-Color Conjecture originated in the minds of Appel and Haken, and this process was in no way facilitated by a computer. The computer was merely used as a tool to check and eliminate many different special cases in which the theorem might (but does not) fail. While not denying the role that computers have played and will continue to play in "case checking," it nevertheless is true that only very rarely, if ever, do mathematicians use computers in the conceptualization stage.

The typical situation encountered is that the calculations necessary to solve a problem are either infinite in extent or so massive that they are even beyond any imaginable computer's capacity. At this point enter the mathematician or the physicist, who "solves" the problem by reducing it to a problem already solved or to a problem requiring so few calculations that a computer is unnecessary.

A prime example of this occurred recently as mathematicians (They were called physicists in the article.) announced the discovery of a technique to solve the quantum chromodynamics (QCD) equations[66]. Previously, only computers could obtain partial and inadequate solutions to the system of equations. Now, after the mathematician's discovery, only paper and pencil is needed to obtain solutions. The computer was of no consequence in obtaining the ultimate breakthrough, except possibly for providing a high level of frustration needed to stimulate the research in the first place!

Certainly in my personal experience, when I am working on a problem and then turn to the keyboard of my computer to begin tapping away, my thought processes stop. Most of my attention is directed to the machine with a proportional loss of ability to think about the problem at hand. This experience may very well be due to my having become "computer literate" after forty years of age, or due to quirks of my own temperament, or perhaps having worked only with pencil and paper during my formative years.

Of the many mathematicians I have informally polled on the subject of using the computer to direct research, very few claim to have found the computer of any use in this regard. This even includes those working in combinatorics. The latter is a field that deals exclusively with whole numbers and counting things that are sometimes difficult to count.

A mathematician friend, who has taken a keen interest in computers and who is able to write computer programs in a number of different languages, happens also to be an active researcher and frequent contributor to mathematical journals. If anyone could have found the computer a useful research tool, it should have been he. In all of his experience, however, he claims only once having arrived at a research result suggested by a computer's numerical output. And even this, he says, was a rather minor and isolated instance.

There are some areas of applied mathematical research for which very powerful computers capable of many megaflops (million floating-point operations per second) have utility. For example, in global weather forecasting most of the mathematical models require massive computational power. Each point among many thousands on a massive grid is dynamically modeled. The computer is at its best when applied to such problems. Other examples are the study of laminar flow over surfaces and acoustical propagation of sound through ocean layers.

It is even conceivable that computer outputs from such problems might lead to the discovery of heretofore-unknown general physical principles. From past experience, however, I believe such occurrences would be few and far between.

COMPUTER ART

What about art on a micro? Yes, that's right, use your PC to create art. Nicholas Negroponte[44], professor of architecture and specializing in computer graphics, has said that "Rarely have two disciplines joined forces seemingly to bring out the worst in each other as have computers and art. ...the results are predominantly bad art and petty programming."

Apparently not everyone agrees with that assessment. A computer program and robotic control that paints are the work of Harold Cohen, 66, a celebrated British artist and, more recently, professor in the visual arts department of the University of California at San Diego who gave up painting more than 20 years ago to see if he could come up with a computer program that could create works of art.

The result was Aaron, a computer program that directs a robotic arm to pour out ink and dye into a cup, grasp a metal brush with a foam pad on the end, and then draw. Aaron is what is called a knowledge-based system. It has no camera or other visual input; all it knows about the world is the programmer's inputs. But the latter is extensive, and for 23 years, Cohen has been honing the rules that drive Aaron.

Although Aaron has no capacity to learn, it can draw an infinite variety of faces, but it is restricted to drawing adult human subjects. Aaron forces observers to confront what it means to create and even to think. But is it art? Aaron's works have been displayed and sold, but most art critics do not believe that real art can come from a computer. As Cohen says, "Art writers run like hell."

CHAPTER 14

COMPUTER TALK

The recent book by John Barry[4] captures the sometimes hilarious and often frustrating invasion of our linguistic psyche by the computer revolutionaries. The function of technobabble is same as that of pig Latin used by children, signals and signs used by inner-city gangs, or military jargon used by members of the armed forces. It is to communicate with members of a well-defined group and to exclude from communication non-members of the group. In this case the group consists of those who work closely and frequently with computers.

Actually there is a darker purpose of technobabble, and that is to deceive. Not since the Vietnam war has there been such a gushing of euphemisms and invention of pseudo-terminology. Remember *Vietnamization, relocation-centers, body counts, limited engagements, incursions, fragging, capturing hearts and minds*, etc.

As long as the function of technobabble is understood, there is no reason to be intimidated by it. Also, it is likely that the more technobabble surrounding a subject, the smaller its content is likely to be.

To be recognized as a legitimate member of the programmers' group one must use exactly the right words in the correct contexts. For example, a programmer does not program, he "codes," and he is not a programmer, he is a "software developer" or "software engineer." He doesn't turn his computer on; he "boots up." He never works on a project; he "supports it." Trying to gain acceptance to the group and to speak otherwise would be like a World War II spy with an English accent trying to penetrate the German high command.

First, there was the basic dichotomy between hardware and software. Hardware is generally built on "cards": the familiar computer boards bristling with chips, transistors, and capacitors. And then there's the "mother board" which integrates all of the cards. The individual cards plug into the motherboard. Software is more ephemeral, but not less important. It is copied into RAM (random access memory) as a series of magnetically encoded zeroes and ones (the bits!). When the computer runs a program, it reads this string of zeroes and ones which translate into whatever the programmer intended: numerical values, a string of alphabetical characters, a colorful graph, or what have you.

After hardware and software came a hybrid, "firmware," software that was burned into a chip. In fact, the line between software and hardware has become very fuzzy. Software can stand in for hardware; that is to say, software can simulate the actions of hardware. The reverse is true as well. Nowadays we have all kinds of wares: *middleware, groupware, zware, UnixWare*, etc. Software descriptions can be very cryptic, usually only an acronym is provided. There are ASCII (pronounced "askey") data, GUIs (pronounced "gooeys"), OODs, RDBs, TCP IPs, and SQLs (pronounced "sequels", ... the list is seemingly endless.

I have a 133-megahertz Pentium PC with 16 megabytes of RAM, a 2.7-gigabyte hard drive, and 256k of pipelined burst cache. I just hope that my pipelined cache, or whatever it is, does not burst.

This is a partial description of my hardware. At least some of this terminology is familiar to most people, even to those who have had no direct experience with computers. Fewer people know the meaning of 133 megahertz (it means 133 million cycles per second) or what RAM stands for (it stands for "random access memory"). And only a small percentage of that group know the details of exactly what 133 megahertz means for the central processing unit (CPU).

I was entertained recently on a trip to our local mega computer store. A short fast talking salesman, Charles, with sales trophy buttons on his lapel rattled off in machine gun fashion the hardware specs of the machine in front of him. “If you’ve only got sixteen megs of SDRAM then you need at least 256k of the pipelined burst cache; unless your RAM is EDO, in that case, since the EDO is working independent of the cache, you can get by with only 128k.”

“Sure,” I said knowingly, “It's just that I’m not sure I have enough CASH to pay for the damn thing.” “That’s OK,” retorted Charles, “Think it over, and come back Monday.” “Will you be here tomorrow afternoon?" I inquired. "The store’s open.” “Nope, on Sundays I’m the minister of a congregation," Charles answered, "come back Monday.”

There is “mainframe architecture” and “client-server architecture.” the latter being in current vogue, although the venerable mainframe is making a comeback. Basically, with the mainframe you have a “dumb terminal” sitting on your desk, and with the client-server you have some computer power sitting in front of you. Therefore, the reasoning goes, the processing is more distributed and tailored to the almighty client. The down side is that the client-server can also be more expensive and difficult to maintain, especially if the clients are geographically spread out.

One major impetus for the ever-expanding computer related jargon is the never-ending stream of software fads. There is an entire vocabulary of euphemisms, acronyms, nouns masquerading as verbs, verbs masquerading as nouns, and other malapropisms. The jargon generally serves to reinforce the mystic of computers. Some of my favorite definitions are:

- **4GLs** = fourth generation languages. Originally referred to one of the object-oriented languages such as C++, Smalltalk, etc. Now it has become associated with a state of mind.
- ***consultant*** = someone who is unemployed. (Consultants are never unemployed; they are said to be “*between assignments.*”)
- ***customer-support analyst*** = salesman
- ***engineer*** = anyone who works with computers, so, for example, as we’ve said, a programmer is a software *engineer,* also a cus-

tomer-support analyst is a *sales engineer*. There are *database* engineers, who are, of course, *information engineers*.

- ***end-user*** = lowest form of human life, someone who uses computers but doesn't really know anything about them.
- ***thin client*** = has nothing whatsoever to do with body fat; it is an end-user client computer (part of the client-server architecture) without much processing power.
- ***support*** = the meaning of this word is so general as to defy definition. Think of it as verbal punctuation.
- ***proprietary*** = keep your cotton-picking hands off! As in the expression: "My code is proprietary!"
- ***data mining*** = similar to coal mining or copper mining except that you do it with data above ground.
- ***information technology (IT)*** = term having no meaning, pure buzzwords.
- ***information technology officer (ITO)*** = new corporate rank, can mean anything from public relations, to human resources to marketing.
- ***UNIX*** = the name of a popular operating system, originally known as *Multix*. At the time Multix was too cumbersome for the available hardware, and so had to be cut back. As someone said, it was made into a "eunuch." Hence the name UNIX was born.

Marketing Talk

The power of language is nowhere more evident than it is in marketing information technology. The right name for software can bring it success in the market place. Take the case of operating systems. That's the software that makes it possible for you the user to interact with the computer and run programs.

Apple computer was the first to launch an icon-based, rather than command-line based, operating system. Then entered Microsoft, who some would say, purloined Apple's system, with their version named

Windows. That name *Windows* somehow linguistically captured what was going on, and propelled Microsoft to market dominance in operating systems for PCs, and for that matter, in most other PC based software.

Ah, yes, and then there's the name Personal Computer, even though we may not think of it as such. It was IBM's genius to call their micros *Personal Computers*, AKA *PC*s. At one stroke IBM made their machines synonymous with all micros. The market advantage from this one act is incalculable. IBM pursued a similar tack with its hardware, allowing the cloning of its PC architecture. The proprietary nature of Apple's hardware actually worked against the company in the larger battle for market share.

CHAPTER 15

COMPUTERS IN THE WORKPLACE

"REAL WORK" IS DONE ONLY AT A COMPUTER TERMINAL.

I recently worked at the headquarters of a large corporation in the Revenue Management Department. This department is responsible for recommending sales strategies to management in order to maximize revenue. The company depends heavily on computers to run its worldwide reservation system as well as other inventory subsystems.

All work, and I mean ALL, is done at a computer terminal. The light switch that I turned on in the morning also sent power to my PC terminal, which left room for little else on my desk. The employees keep track of time spent on projects by means of a computer program, appropriately named "timecard." Never mind that running this program and maintaining it takes much more time than filling out an old-fashioned paper timecard.

During fleeting moments of insight, some managers in the Revenue Management Department have given thought to breaking away from the department's entrenched computer culture. This is a culture that doesn't even admit that any real work could be done other than at a keyboard. Unfortunately, none of these moments of insight has borne fruit. Consequently, the company has developed no "in house" operations research capability, which translates into an inability to do anything except to move data from one place to another.

The company pays for this mindless notion that all work is done at the keyboard. Indeed, they pay heavily by having to go to high-priced outside contractors not only to develop their revenue management systems, but to perform many other relatively simple tasks as well. The work that the outside contractors perform is not difficult, but it does involve thinking, the kind of thinking that is not done at a keyboard.

DOING "REAL WORK" AT A COMPUTER WORK-STATION

A large "thinktank" in the Washington D.C. area kept log-in and log-out time records of all its employees having access to the company's computer systems. A glance at these records would tell managers for what periods and for how long individual employees were "logged on" to the computer system. This information was not sought for the purpose of snooping; on the contrary, awards were given to those employees who recorded the most "logged-on" time.

David, aware of this monitoring by management, simply got into the habit of staying logged on as much as possible, even occasionally leaving himself logged on over night. He even went a step further and wrote a computer program that continuously wrote messages to the video screen giving the appearance to anyone who happened to walk by his workstation that serious work was in progress. Needless to say, the employees, who knew him to be otherwise lazy and not especially bright, were amused when David received the company's award for "Hardest Working Employee."

This story, while certainly not flattering to the management of this particular institution, does illustrate a mindset that is common to most companies of the "high-tech" variety: Excepting possibly managerial activities, only *real* work is done at the computer workstation.

One reason managerial activities are excepted is that the managers themselves tend to be older than the rest of the workforce, and therefore probably did not grow up with computers and may not be even computer literate. So obviously this group would except itself when making judgments about work output. Also, not knowing much about computers makes it easier to be duped into this mindset in the first place.

What do computers do in the workplace? The short answer is that they run "applications." *Application* is an industry code word for any computer program that performs some office task. Ninety nine percent of applications used are word processing programs, spreadsheet generators, or card catalogue type schedulers.

Initially, Intel Corporation was justifiably unconcerned when it was discovered that there was a mathematically significant flaw in the floating-point arithmetic of its new chip. Intel knew that a relatively small fraction of applications require any mathematical computations whatsoever. And an even smaller fraction of a fraction require those calculations to be accurate. Market psychology forced Intel to give in and replace the flawed chips. Customers were insulted that their applications might be thought so trivial as not to require the designed accuracy of the chip.

The Payoff from Computerization

The computerization of the workplace can hardly be over estimated. The Bureau of Labor Statistics[84] reports that for 1993 a total of over 51 million US workers used computers on the job. That represented almost 46 percent of the workforce. The workplace uses of the computer ranged from word-processing and spreadsheets to inventory and data base maintenance.

What has been the payoff from this computerization of the workplace? There is strong evidence to support the conclusion that the revolution has not brought about the much touted "leisure society" overnight. According to a Harris survey, the amount of leisure time enjoyed by the average US citizen shrunk by a staggering 37 per cent between 1973 and 1989. During the same time the average work-week, including travel-to-work time, grew from about 41 hours to almost 47 hours[27]. There are other indicators as well that Americans are working longer and harder.

Contrary to naive predictions that the microchip would reduce employment, there is every indication that the new technology has created jobs, although there will be lengthy and painful periods of adjustment for certain groups of workers. The jobs created are largely within the high-tech sector itself, and this sector is relatively small compared to total employment.

What about gains in productivity as a result of computerization? Again, the indications are that it has not happened overnight. For example, in the US financial industry, which was among the first to automate operations, capital productivity in US banks began to decline steadily after 1958 with the onset of computerization and continued to decline until the 80s! By 1980 half of capital expenditure went to computers and peripherals!

Landauer[38] presents the results of several econometric analyses of the productivity effects of informational technology over a broad sector of American service and manufacturing industries. Most of the findings are surprisingly negative: the analyses revealed a slightly negative effect of computerization on productivity! As Landauer points out, this may be because the productivity measured does not account for intangibles such as the common good and quirks of customer preferences. As an example, he mentions the very popular ATM services that almost all banks now provide. The cost of providing the service may not be offset by an increase in productivity, but customers overwhelmingly prefer ATMs to human tellers, even if the waiting line is greater for the ATM.

One might reasonably ask why business investment in information technology is accelerating given the lack-luster returns. I think the primary reason for this is the unreasonably good reputation in the public mind that computers enjoy. Although the over-all return on investment is poor, there have been spectacular success stories.

The cost of implementing a computerized revenue management system in the company where I recently worked came to about five million dollars. Management estimated that this single automated system yields an additional $100 million in revenue. Perhaps you might think that this estimate of additional revenue is inflated. Even so, assuming it's inflated by a factor of two or three, and you take into account the annual cost of maintaining the system, the return on investment for that particular system is clearly fabulous. The benefit to the company of this system, however, is almost certainly offset by the high cost of other "white elephant" computer systems that return little if anything.

It seems reasonable to suppose that it takes time for the new computer technology to impact productivity. Initial computerization leads to decreased capital productivity and profitability. Time is needed to separate the wheat from the chaff. It will not likely be until the 21st century before accumulated experience with producing and using computers will pay dividends.

What about the payoff from office automation? This must surely be an area where computerization has made a big difference. No, it hasn't. US Bureau of Labor Statistics figures show that overall office productivity in the US is no higher than it was in the late 1960s. Naturally, capital expenditures on computers have zoomed[7].

The tendency of productivity rates to dip or flatten at workplaces after the introduction of information technology is known to economists as the *productivity paradox*. Investments in information technology began to take off in the mid-1970s. Thereafter, curves of productivity in manufacturing began to rise somewhat. In the service-industry, however, where 80 percent of information technology investment has been made, productivity growth has fallen[10].

My experience with getting mathematics papers typed is anecdotal, but it may offer a clue as to why office productivity hasn't gone up after computerization. Before word processors and laser printers, technical papers were typed on electric typewriters allowing only very minor corrections-a few words at most, unless one were to retype the entire page. Consequently, a manuscript (hand-written, of course) was carefully proofread before being handed over to the typist. Any significant alteration to the manuscript at a later time was met with raised eyebrows and possibly dirty looks.

Nowadays one hands anything over to the typist, knowing that alterations, additions, deletions are relatively easy to make. Therefore, a technical paper is typically repeatedly revised and printed out. Incidentally, this accounts for why **more** paper is used because of computers, not less. Although computerization has not resulted in a more productive office, the author may have been freed from meticulous proofreading. Is this a benefit or a loss? I'm not sure.

Personal Digital Assistants (PDAs) may be an important work tool of the future: the perfect secretary who never asks to be taken to lunch. The principal feature of these machines is their presumed ability to recognize and process handwriting to the "notepad." To do this with a useful degree of precision and reliability is a very ambitious technological goal, one that will probably be achieved, but not in the very near future.

E-MAIL AND INTRA-OFFICE COMMUNICATIONS

Nowadays, e-mail, or electronic mail, is the vehicle of choice for workplace communication. It is also the single most important utility available on the Internet. Users of e-mail derisively refer to old-fashioned United States Post Office letter mail as "snail mail."

E-mail enables your supervisor in a cube 15 feet away to talk to you without actually speaking near your face. Since he may be a shy but demanding sort, this form of communication serves him well. In fact, he may spend most of the day writing e-mail correspondence, as well as correspondence using other inter-office and intra-office communication software such as Lotus Notes.

Somehow the use of e-mail allows for extensive communication having little content. Instead, it is an endless archiving of small events and administrative trivia having little or no consequence aside from marking the passage of time.

One is reminded of the man who made the Guinness Book of World Records for having kept the longest continuous personal diary. He spent a large fraction of his waking hours making new entries in his diary. The smallest event was dutifully recorded. It seems to me that the sad part of his story was that he recorded no new ideas, thoughts, or words. The same may be said of e-mail and the like. This software does not facilitate the generation of ideas or thoughts. It probably distracts from the genesis of such.

COORDINATION THEORY

An age-old question is: how can people and machines work together to create a better world? A new interdisciplinary field called "coordination theory" has been invented at the Massachusetts Institute of Technology. The idea is to develop a scientific theory that would explain how the activities of separate players, both individuals and machines, can be coordinated.

Coordination theory explores computer and communications systems to help people work together in small or large groups. Successful commercial versions of coordination technologies are already appearing as "GroupWare", such as Lotus Notes, and "client/server" based computer networks.

In April 1990 MIT opened the Center for Coordination Science at the Sloan School of Management[79]. Although the opening of the center suggests that coordination theory is new, in reality it has been studied for several decades.

Anatol W. Holt, chief technical officer of Coordination Technology Inc., in Trumbull, Conn., has pioneered a concept known as "coordination mechanics," a study of coordination that emphasizes task-oriented relationships among people working together. A key part of Holt's theory is the use of Petri nets, a mathematical approach to distributed processes.

As the 'information society' we are entering a new phase. There is an increasing trend toward decentralization of both computer and human activity. Coordination theory may well shape organizations of the future. Traditional hierarchy structures may become less important or even disappear altogether and be replaced with networks. Management as we know it today, may become invisible or have its functions dispersed throughout a network.

In corporate America the people who work most intensively with computers are generally segregated in a niche of the company known as the "Systems Division." These are the people whose worth to the company is measured in terms of their individual "skill sets." The "Systems Division" is generally the division lowest on the corporate totem pole. The systems people take a back seat to the business side of the house. They are viewed as a service group to carry out the bidding of people whose knowledge of computers is far less. Rarely, if ever, does corporate direction originate in the systems division.

The Dumbing Down of America

To the uninitiated it might seem plausible that the rise of the prominence of computers in the workplace should have fostered an enhanced growth of intellectual and technical skills among those who work in the industry. Nothing could be further from the truth. In fact there is a strong association between the "dumbing-down" phenomenon and the computer culture itself.

Forest Gump could just as easily have been a computer nerd. He's smart enough to program computers-at least on a certain level, and certainly smart enough to fill one of the many computer-related positions we see so widely advertised in the employment section of the Sunday paper.

Many of the titles are lofty sounding: UNIX Systems Administrator, Software Test Manager, VAX Systems Manager, GUI (pronounced "gooey" and standing for "graphical user interface") Developer, Information Specialist, Data Base Administrator (DBA). These are a few random titles pulled from the Sunday Washington Post.

Sounds like you'd need at least a Ph.D. just to get the job! Not by a long shot. It's true that for almost all of these jobs, if you had a Ph.D., you would be over-qualified for the job. For example, a UNIX Systems Administrator is a guy who has memorized the UNIX commands, can boot the machine, do backups, allocate machine resources, keep the users informed of the machine's status, and perform basic housekeeping duties.

All of these activities, while they may appear highly technical and complex to an outsider, require little or no advanced language ability, reasoning, or creativity. Now, I do not wish to disparage the duties of a hard working UNIX Systems Administrator. I am sure that there are many very smart and talented people performing such duties, just as there are very smart and talented people driving buses. It's just that the duties of the latter group are more transparent and less easily confused with intellectual, deductive, or analytical skills.

The New Work Order

The computer revolution has spawned a whole new industry, namely, the behemoth technical recruiter industry. In the 1980s high-tech corporations, deluged with resumes, decided to hire independent firms to handle the unpleasant task of winnowing out the best. Thus were born the "body shops." The "bodies" are the construction workers and housekeepers of the computer industry. In earlier times these people would have been farmers, shopkeepers, and seamstresses.

It's called the "New Work Order." The body shops collect resumes with the right buzzwords and use them to try to fill "requirements" (the "recks") demanded by the human resources people of high-tech firms. The contractors, called "consultants," are then forced through a ritual of sometimes hundreds of phone screenings, during which the buzzwords are repeated, followed by perhaps one or two flesh and blood interviews, at which the buzzwords are repeated still one more time. If a job offer results, it is most likely a job as a "temp" or "temp-to-perm," during which status the consultant is an employee of the body shop paid an hourly rate with few or no benefits.

While many jobs in the computer industry are high paying, most are not. In order to hold costs down, hiring is focused on the young, who, by the way, having grown up in the culture, happen to have better computer skills anyway. The ads often say something like "one to three years experience desired." This really translates into "AT MOST three years experience." Although the companies are alert to charges of age and sex discrimination, and when asked state that years of experience required are always minimums, everyone knows that is not the case.

Computer skills no longer guarantee employment. The six-figure-paying programming jobs of the early eighties are mostly gone. It's no longer necessary to write code in an arcane assembly language-one of the high level object oriented languages like C++ is more in demand.

To make matters worse, coding tasks are easily exported to Eastern Europe, the Far East, and India. Mastech Systems Corporation, a software development company based in Pittsburgh, PA, advertises in its brochure, "Mastech's off-shore software teams in India can take advantage of the 10-hour time difference by using your in-house computer resources during off-peak hours...You can reduce your software development and maintenance costs to as low as $14-20 per hour, which in most cases results in savings of 50-70% over US-based rates."

Programming tasks in the US are increasingly being done on a piecework basis by "temps." In the Washington D.C. area "body shops" are springing up everywhere. More than 10 pages of classified ads in every Sunday paper seek temporary employees to fill their "requirements."

On the positive side, the relative abundance in some geographic areas of computer jobs has been a conduit to better opportunity for those with little or no higher education. These jobs in general pay higher than minimum wage jobs, but often do not require much more training. The jobs that have been eliminated by computers have been more than offset in number by the jobs created by computers.

The cliché that we will all be replaced by computers is patently false, just as the claim that computers would eliminate the need for paper. Indeed, the widespread use of computers has increased paper consumption. Everyone must keep a "hard copy" of each of his or her important files in case of a disk "crash," even if backups of the files are kept on "floppies," since they too are subject to catastrophic failure. In any case, most files with the possible exception of e-mail files are eventually turned into paper copies.

The computer workplace today is a world without books. Indeed the notion of "book" seems anathema to the workplace. Even the usual office dictionary or Thesaurus has disappeared. Almost all systems have on-line look-up libraries and spell checkers. There is one small exception to the "no-book rule," and that is only for the relatively few who write computer programs. This group has a need to learn computer language syntax and form.

One small way that the computer industry has fostered the creation of additional jobs (and also used more paper) is seen in the growth of the computer-book economy. Anyone who has visited any of the commercial bookstores lately has seen the large section devoted to computer books-mostly paperback with wildly colored covers, big thick heavy tomes with titles like: C++ Programming (800+ pages), Sybase Developers Guide (700 pages), Visual Basic for Dummies (435 pages). As one might guess from the number of pages, the style of writing is not dense, and copious examples are frequently provided.

Over the past few years, I have watched as Reiter's, an old established technical book store in Washington D.C., has grown a computer book section that now occupies fully a prominent one-third of the store's floor space.

Since students generally do not graduate knowing all of the computer languages demanded by the workplace, they must learn them later on their own. These books, although dull, are generally well written and serve an important function in the workplace. Considering the amount of paper in them, they seem reasonably priced at roughly between $25 and $50.

Computer Games in the Workplace

Although computer games are perhaps less relevant in the adult world than in the world of children, they have attained a presence there nevertheless. Anyone familiar with the day-to-day operations of a modern office has occasion to observe workers busily playing *solitaire* (probably the favorite time killer) for the gals or *submarine* for the guys during breaks, and sometimes, heaven forbid, on company time. Indeed, in some state offices the problem has become acute.

Recently, the governor of Virginia, George Allen, was forced to decree that state workers could no longer play computer games on their office machines--even on breaks. The games would have to go!

Computer Related Injuries

One would think that the use of computers would entail the least possible risk of physical injury among all professions. Surprisingly, that is not the case. In fact, the field of ergonomics has come into being to address questions that relate to the interaction of human with machine.

The keyboard and terminal have proven fertile sources of human physical and psychological misery. Long-term keyboard use has led to carpal tunnel syndrome, a painful affliction of the joints of the fingers caused by repeated keystrokes while holding the hands together in the standard forward typing position. Other afflictions, often of the back, arise due to the prolonged sitting position at the keyboard.

The computer industry has responded to the carpal tunnel syndrome problem with a futuristic looking keyboard rising in the middle and curved in three dimensions. The strange looking furniture used for kneeling at the keyboard, rather than for sitting in the usual manner, is intended to relieve stress on the back.

The low-level electromagnetic radiation put out by the video terminal itself is suspect in contributing to a number of ailments. Since the fetus is particularly susceptible to the environmental effects of radiation, pregnant women are advised by many physicians to limit their time spent at a workstation.

There are radiation-inhibiting filters available which fit over the video screen and presumably eliminate at least some of the electromagnetic radiation. The bottom line is that data implicating or absolving video radiation in harming humans is insufficient and inconclusive. It is perhaps this uncertainty that carries a psychological penalty.

Undoubtedly, the greatest health risk caused by computers is the physical inactivity and inertia they engender. Their use demands complete physical inactivity, making a "walk in the park" to clear one's head even more important after a long period at the keyboard.

Computer Scientists on Computers in the Workplace

In an interview after receiving the Allan Turing award in 1994 Raj Reddy was asked to offer advice for corporate information systems managers. His reply was, "They have to put the infrastructure in place-a PC on every desk, even the janitor's. No exception. And they have to be networked. The second thing is training. You might be using the computer only for word processing and not know it can be used for scheduling, planning, e-mail, project management and so forth."

Apparently, the workplace has already heeded Reddy's plea. A project I recently worked on is typical. The government let a contract to develop an automated data processing (ADP) system at the offices of a large federal bureaucracy in Washington, D.C. The process by which the retirement entitlements and benefits of the approximately two and a half million retiring federal workers are calculated is still manually done-a laborious process which takes approximately 107 days for each worker. When completed this system is supposed to improve this time to 107 seconds. Assuming all goes well, it's supposed to be completed in about four years.

This project has roughly thirty networked PCs with access to a "mainframe" computer. People spend all day sending one another e-mail messages and making up schedules for endless meetings in which the development of the project's software is discussed. Do you think time is being wasted on all this networked garbage? You bet! But at least it gives the workers something to do and a sense, albeit a false sense, of accomplishment. All the networking activity covers up weak management and a host of other sins.

And here's an update on this project. The client, even though it is a large government agency, wised up and decided to declare a "stop work order" while it decided what to do. It finally realized that two and one-half years and tens of millions of taxpayers' dollars have gone by and there's very little to show for the investment. If the computer revolution is a war, a big battle has just been lost!

And what's coming in the corporate world? Reddy believes the answer is "intelligent agents." Roughly speaking, an intelligent agent is a computer program looking over your shoulder to spot trouble before it develops. For example, he envisions an agent to look over everyone's expenditures and alert designated human agents to any situation out of the ordinary. So much for good old-fashioned embezzlement!

According to Reddy, "We are all getting swamped with information. Agents will monitor things, read and understand content, filter the information and tell you, 'This is important; you'd better attend to it now.' These exist now in a primitive form [in commercial electronic-mail filters, story filters used by new wire services, etc.], but they need to get smarter."

If intelligent "agents" are coming to the corporate world as predicted by Reddy, "client/server" based programs are what is already here and under the most intense development. These are rather large chunks of software and hardware that allow remote users, AKA the "client," to query a large centrally located data base, AKA the "server," receive answers back and perhaps make appropriate changes to the data base.

Client-server has been over hyped, and in many instances has not delivered on its promises. That's why the big mainframe is making a comeback. The cover of a leading IT trade journal recently trumpeted: Tony Bennett and Big Iron (the mainframes) Are Back!

Most important, client-server in many cases has proven to be much more expensive to implement than anticipated. Over all, it may be a more robust architecture, but it can also be a huge nuisance to maintain, since processing goes on at sometimes hundreds of remote sites. A remedy for this problem that is being talked about a lot lately is the so-called "thin-client" architecture. This just means that almost all of the required processing is carried out at the server end, so the client's machine only submits requests to the server and receives data back from the server for display.

The telecommunications industry is a heavy user of client-server systems, as are the financial and travel industries. Look at the most actively traded issues on the NASDAQ stock exchange. Most of them are high-tech stocks, and during the last twelve months many have been companies whose principal product is a data base engine or the network software or hardware to built a client/server system and custom design it to fit a customer's particular needs: Sybase, which bills itself as the Enterprise Client/Server Company, and Oracle, Sybase's principal competitor; Cisco, manufacturer of network hardware; Novell and Lotus, popular networking software, are also frequently on the "most actively traded" list.

To the uninitiated this industry may certainly seem high-tech; certainly the product it produces is very useful to the business community, but in the colloquialism of the time, it's not rocket science. Nevertheless, at the moment these activities are at the core of the so-called information revolution. In a few years or less the approaches that industry takes to information technology almost certainly will change completely.

What course will the industry take after client-server is ancient history? It's likely to have something to do with wireless computer hookups. Now when you're on the Internet or networked at the office, there's a physical connection (usually a telephone line) between your computer and the server and your co-workers. When wireless computer hookups become reality, the door will be opened for brand new networking architectures. These architectures are likely to be even more diffuse than the present ones.

Chapter 16

Information Superhighway

Alvin Toeffler has described Three Great Waves: the transition from a hunter-gatherer society to an agricultural one, the industrial revolution, and the third being the one we are presumably in, namely, the information revolution. If that is the case, then the information superhighway must certainly be of tremendous importance to mankind.

The Vision: The Knowledge Navigator

In describing a future-generation Macintosh computer John Scully presented[58] a widely held vision of the information superhighway. The Knowledge Navigator is a wonderful fantasy machine allowing you to steer through various windows and menus opening galleries, stacks, and museums galore. You won't have to search through the stacks of libraries-the world's largest library will exist on your desktop or your lap. Indeed, the voyages of Jules Verne will pale by comparison.

This machine would invite you deep inside the secrets of the great resources, interpreting and explaining-converting vast quantities of information into personalized and understandable knowledge. You will see images in full color, high-definition, television-quality images, and full pages of text, graphics, and computer-generated animation. You will hear high-fidelity sound, speech synthesis, and speech recognition. This was then and remains so today the vision of the information superhighway.

To support this grand future Macintosh, Scully boldly asserts, "By the early twenty-first century, all scholarly knowledge will be fully digitized, electronically sitting in computers around the world." At the time of his writing the twenty-first century was thirteen years away. Today it is less than three. Scully's remarks imply a fundamental misunderstanding of both scholarly knowledge and technology. Indeed, one is reminded of the old Indian superstition that if I can capture an image of my enemy in some medium, whether it is clay or film, then I have absolute power over him.

Almost as if to negate these grandiose prognostications, Scully goes on to write:

"Innovation will never take root in our society unless a revolution in learning begins at the start of one's education. If we had the Navigator tomorrow it would, therefore, change nothing. Wide-spread changes, particularly in education, must first occur if there is to be a new renaissance." (Italics are mine.)

Scully's remarks are so much marketing hype-the kind of stuff marketing guys have been saying since the dawn of time. Moreover, the marketplace now recognizes that fact. If Apple's software and hardware designers could have delivered on a fraction of Scully's promises, the company would have done better. Recently, the company's fortunes have fallen into the hands of more pragmatic leaders.

THE REALITY: THE INTERNET

The coming of the Internet has brought the world still closer to the "world village" concept. On June 4, 1995, Chinese police on patrol during the anniversary of the bloody Tiananmen Square revolt failed to detect a Statue of Liberty-like "goddess of democracy" standing beside the slogan: "It is painful to recall, but it is never to be forgotten." The message eluded police because it appeared on the Internet[76e].

The Internet, like the facsimile machine and television before it, is another avenue to disseminate information to large numbers of people. It homogenizes ideas, and makes it more difficult for dictatorship to exclude impure thoughts. At the time of the Communist takeover of China in 1949, Mao said that power came from the barrel of a gun. These days, he might have said that it comes from the keyboard of a computer.

A recent news article contained a description of ARPA's (Advanced Research Projects Agency) computer control room at the Arlington, Virginia, headquarters dubbed the Enterprise. Picture the computer banks with blinking lights and the full-wall video screen on the starship Enterprise of TV fame and you pretty much have the idea of the place. Information from the Internet can be projected onto the huge screen allowing the people there to be in touch (wired) with the hundreds and thousands of people logged-on at remote sites around the world.

The Internet, perhaps ARPA's best known invention, is a network of computers belonging to private companies, universities, government agencies, and individuals. The global village! The information superhighway! When the Internet began in 1969; it was known, quite naturally, as the ARPANET. Actually a contract was awarded to Bolt, Baranek and Newman (BBN) of Cambridge, Massachusetts to develop the ARPANET. It began as a link connecting four locations: the University of California at Los Angeles, the University of California at Santa Barbara, the University of Utah, and Stanford Research Institute.

Since its inception, ARPANET, which technically doesn't exist anymore, has developed into a worldwide packet switching network connecting hundreds of dissimilar computers. The Internet, as it has come to be known, includes the old ARPANET, the National Science Foundation Network (NSFNET), the Computer Science Network (CSNET), the Because It's Time Network (BITNET), and the network for military traffic (MILNET).

Last year, immediately after his lecture announcing a proof of the famous Fermat's Last Theorem, news of Andrew Wiles' accomplishment together with some of the details were flashed around the world on the Internet and read by hundreds if not thousands. That event illustrated the extent to which the "bandwidth" of the Internet exceeds that of, say, the telephone.

Certainly no one can deny the tremendous popularity of the Internet; its appeal has been almost universal. By and large its appeal is due to the innate human enjoyment of idle chatter, endless idle chatter, particularly by the very young. Even scientists, however, can be guilty of enjoying frivolous and superficial dialogue, as anyone who has attended university faculty meetings can attest.

A generation earlier some of these people engaged in the more noble sport of letter writing. I say more noble because composing letters seemed to demand a higher level of thoughtfulness and more careful attention to such details as spelling and grammar.

Most Internet users have been associated with one or more of the topic-oriented bulletin board systems (BBS). There were about 60,000 BBSs in the US in 1993 each consisting of from a dozen to several hundred or sometimes even thousands of participants. There are BBSs devoted to raising pet snakes, civil war history, stock market investments, daytime soap operas, and kinky sex.

Even the President and Vice-President of the United States now have their own e-mail addresses. The present administration was particularly keen on upgrading the communications facilities of the executive quarters. You can now address an e-letter to President@Whitehouse, or Vice.President@Whitehouse. I suppose some staffer has the responsibility to look at incoming e-mail and respond appropriately.

Enthusiastic governmental predictions for the Internet sound remarkably like predictions made for the future of cable TV made twenty-five years ago. The National Science Foundation predicted that cable TV would offer:..."Public access channels available to individual citizens and community groups ...New services to individual subscribers, such as televised college courses and continuing education classes in the home[2]." As it turned out, cable TV came to support very little of this lofty stuff.

Communication on the Internet can be, and often is, anonymous. The electronic letters (e-mail) are more ephemeral and superficial and are almost never intended to be reread or even retained in the computer's memory. They are best described as "spoken writing:" quick tidbits of information not intended to be digested but to be passed on to others wired to the same network.

My first experience with e-mail was trivial but probably typical. Messages received within my building were of the type: "Someone with a red Honda, license plate ZYE-496, left his lights on," or "There's a brown-bag lunch-lecture this Thursday on wavelets." Until I learned of the cost of wiring the building and monthly charges for access to the net, I thought that a great deal of money was being saved in long-distance telephone charges.

Messages sent back and forth to other research centers were more or less the written equivalent of spoken conversations. Rarely was any e-letter intended to convey an important scientific or engineering conclusion. That was always reserved for the printed or handwritten page sent through the regular mail. Interestingly enough, any contractual matters, and certainly anything that might come from an attorney, were handled through traditional channels.

What's on the information super highway? According to Richard Leiby[41] the answer is a lot of lowbrow culture. Anyone exploring the principal branches of the computer network, e.g. CompuServe, World Wide Web (WWW), America-on-Line, etc., will find a landscape littered with trash, promotional spots, and audio-video files of dubious value. The previously reserved domain of the academics has become a crowded raceway of 20 million or more users, most of whom are, to say the least, not versed in the scientific method: discussion groups devoted to TV shows in which fans exchange bizarre theories, Hollywood gossip, and just plain porn.

I recently asked a manager at America-on-Line who AOL's major competitors were. At the top of the list was not one of the other on-line services but rather CABLE TV! The fact that AOL's major competitor is cable TV, rather than, say, the opera or ballroom dancing serves to benchmark the services provided better than anything I can think of.

College kids are now paying to have their Internet accounts locked out! At the University of Maryland a new campus support group called "Caught in the Web" counsels students spending too much time on computers[76i]. Half of the dropout students at some universities are dropping out because of their addiction to computers. In earlier times these same students would have dropped out as a result of an addiction to playing bridge or pool, or perhaps as a result of an obsession with operating a ham-radio station.

Although I do believe that cigarettes are addictive, I don't believe that computers are. A similar thing goes on in the workplace. Both there and at the university campuses much of the time spent with computers is wasteful and frivolous. These instruments can be time sinks, a means to postpone or to avoid work altogether.

There are also computer network gangs! Masters of Deception (MOD), kids (hackers) hang out together in cyberspace and try to break into local area networks such as the TRW network. They should be sentenced to college! There is even a book about these gangs entitled *Masters of Deception, the kids that ruled cyberspace*. These multitudes have the effect of clogging and slowing the global computer network-as happened recently during a Rolling Stones "multicast" of live concert audio and video over the Internet.

On a more positive note perhaps, the Internet has become as essential to many students' social life as the telephone. They use it to flirt, discuss homework with fellow students, spread the word about parties, and stay in touch with relatives back home. Kevin Hsu, who heads a student computer organization in College Park, said, "These days, if some guy doesn't have an e-mail address, it's almost shocking."

The more serious aficionados of the Internet create their very own "home page," a kind of billboard-scrapbook allowing the creator to advertise to the world his or her family photos, philosophical musings, and random trivial thoughts. Stunningly narcissistic, the home pages are becoming popular on college campuses across the nation-even among students not majoring in science or studying computers.

The lonely and often introverted people who put their "home-pages" on the net for all to peruse are wistfully seeking friends and admirers. Unfortunately, most of the feedback they get is trivial and not likely to shore up their sagging self-images. In any case, such electronic cruisings almost never result in flesh and blood relationships.

Not just the lonely and introverted are creating home pages. Each of the 1996 presidential hopefuls has created his own home page. These are cameo glimpses of the candidate carefully crafted to be astute political advertisements. The proverbial "hat in the ring" has been replaced by "home page on the net." No serious candidate can afford to forgo exposure in cyberspace.

A computer vandal or vandals recently broke into the Justice Department's home page. Remember such "home pages" are essentially public relations billboards in cyberspace, which attempt to cast in the best possible light the charter, goals, and accomplishments of the organization. This time the vandals altered the organization's title to read: "United States Department of Injustice." Also a picture of Adolf Hitler complete with swastikas was inserted together with selected pornography!

Access to the Internet is free to students, but not for universities buying the hardware, laying the cable and wiring dorm rooms. At the University of Maryland, where there are more than 20,000 users, equipment costs were more than $2 million, and annual costs for modems to connect the computers to telephone lines are $400,000.

Heavy traffic at peak hours results in busy signals for people trying to log on to the network. Friday nights are especially bustling with everyone sending e-mail messages back and forth trying to figure out where the action is. The real cost is not so much the dollar cost as it is a waste of time.

"CyberSurfing," one of many new words coined by the revolution, captures the drift of what is happening on the World Wide Web. For the second year in a row, Cygnus Support, a small software company in Mountain View, California, has plugged its Christmas tree into the Internet. CyberSurfers can view photos of it and vote on whether the "Boring Blinking White Lights," "Less Boring Color Lights" or "Tacky Bubble Lights" should be turned on or off -- and every 15 minutes the lights adjust to reflect the latest ballots. During the first 10 days of polling, more than 4,000 people recorded their votes on this important issue.

Does this sound too trivial? If so, you might consider something more important like monitoring a coffee pot in Cambridge or a coke machine at Stanford to see whether they are empty or full-all from far away at your keyboard at home. Why do such a trivial and inane thing? Because it's there, and thanks to the interactive World Wide Web you can do just that and more! All of this goes to show that the technology that has given us the information superhighway has also created a highway of detritus.

CyberBanking

First Virtual Holdings Inc. bills itself as "the world's first electronic merchant banker." Based in Arlington, Virginia, First Virtual is attempting to process Internet financial transactions that would allow you to shop in cyberspace. First Virtual doesn't rely on encryption to fend off hackers; instead, its system keeps your credit card number off the Internet entirely. You open the account by telephone and use an e-mail password to okay purchases.

At the moment First Virtual only provides a link between buyers and sellers of information-based products: software, games, recipes, videos, etc.-anything that can be downloaded or transmitted. Those who've tried First Virtual's services find it easier to order these products by just picking up the phone and dialing an 800 number.

Legislation intended to foster the Clinton Administration during its first two years has pushed the development of the information highway[43]. Legislation for the National Information Infrastructure was declared dead in Congress, at least temporarily. A bill passed by the House of Representatives included language directing the Federal Communications Commission to require communications companies to offer network access to schools at "preferential rates." The bill died, however, in the Senate. Some expect a similar bill to pass early in the next Congress. The outcome is that due to uncertainties in future regulation, telecommunications companies may delay making the investments needed to develop to so-called National Information Infrastructure.

Eleven-year-old Neal Pettingill takes temperature and rainfall readings at the base of a flagpole outside Jamestown Elementary School in Arlington, Virginia as part of the Global Learning and Observations to Benefit the Earth (GLOBE) program. This is the sort of program that resonates with Vice President Gore, who has made computer communications and environmental issues two of his top priorities.

GLOBE is a hands-on science project that has children measuring weather, geographic and biological conditions in their schools' yards to help scientists study environmental changes on the planet. The students then log on to the Internet and record their measurements, which are in turn accessed by scientists. Calling the students "pioneers," Gore told them they soon would be able to communicate with students around the world and interact with their peers.

Here are some reasons to be wired into the Internet via one of the popular network browsers. The advantages are:

- You can dig into the world's biggest, fastest library. Being on-line provides instant, global access to experts and information, via bulletin boards, roundtables and new groups-and the library is always open. Delphi, CompuServe, America On Line, Lexis, ... the list of on-line services is extensive. The article[37] offers the caveat: "...information services are increasingly patrolled by hucksters, blowhards, and self-appointed experts."

• You can take better control of your health care. For example, a person can obtain valuable medical information, even a second opinion on a diagnosis, via on-line bulletin boards. Then there is always the psychological advantage of being able to communicate with fellow sufferers and share experiences.

That all may be true, but this benefit could prove dangerous. Recently, word passed around the net that a drug normally used by epileptics had a restorative effect on those suffering from ALS (Lou Gehrig's disease). It was estimated that fully one-third of ALS sufferers in the United States obtained the drug and administered dosages to themselves. No clinical trials or research whatsoever had been done to verify the drug's effects on ALS.

• You can travel on the inside track. What this means is that you can do what the people do who make the travel arrangements over computer lines. They have instant access to all the possible choices, presumably the cheapest and best travel bargains, therefore you will too, if you are on-line. And if you believe that, there's a bridge....

• You can connect with other collectors and enthusiasts. This advantage is self-explanatory.

• You can enjoy role-playing and strategy games. You can use your computer to access a world, nay a universe, of dungeons and dragons; all the games you've even heard of and many more you have not.

• You can be your own market adviser and monitor. You can get on-line stock quotations and business information of every type. Beware! Many scam artists selling bogus securities and talking up all sorts of rickety investment schemes are infiltrating the on-line world. The Securities Exchange Commission is just starting to crack down on these cyberspace crooks.

• You can ride the cyberspace gravy train. Use on-line services to find clients, vendors, partners, etc. It's a marketing tool.

• Explore your roots and meet new relations. Computer dating. Need I say more? Cybersex? I don't think so.

• You can stay in touch. E-mail is cheaper than long-distance telephoning...if you don't count your hardware and software costs. CompuServe and America Online handle e-mail best, although newcomer eWorld matches them in ease of use.

There are six activities that will not be enhanced by going online:

• You won't develop rich networks of relationships via on-line "chat-rooms." This gets to the heart of the weakness of being wired: it is entertainment, but it's superficial and not likely to result in anything concrete.

• You will not bank via an on-line service. You don't need a computer to bank on-line, use your telephone, stupid!

• You will probably not hob-nob with celebrities. Celebrities, particularly the smart ones, have better things to do than to go on-line and chat.

• You won't bask in multimedia features like sound, movies, and animation. Again, you don't need a computer for this; you've got your TV with generally inexpensive cable.

• You won't play real-time arcade-style games. It's simply too expensive now.

• You won't do your shopping on-line. Once again, there are other avenues for access to merchandise viewing (TV, catalogues) and ordering (your telephone, stupid!).

The Internet has certainly not reached the stage that it may be used as a full-blown research library. Even with the help of powerful computers, the typical Internet search takes too long to be practical for many students and even for faculty members. Although electronic browsers, searching tools, and scores of informal indexes support the network, these tools are fragmented so that it takes all but the expert considerable time to zero in on particular sources.

Most of the problem is undoubtedly due to the explosive growth of the Internet. Someone likened the situation to a library where all the books have been donated by patrons, placed randomly on the shelves with no call numbers, and people can move the books around from shelf to shelf whenever they wish.

Projects are underway at several universities to address the massive management and organizational problems connected with making the Internet an efficient highway to information.

Academic publishing in the multi-media hypertext area has lagged behind commercial publishing, but apparently the reasons for this are lack of technical expertise and equipment, in short, lack of money rather than a lack of commitment. Among researchers, some believe that using hypertext is not unlike doing research in the library, only faster and more efficient. More connections can be made by searching on key words.

Mosaic, an information highway server, was the first major application in the hypertext environment. A hypertext user can choose his own path through the work, pointing and clicking on whatever strikes his interest. Some, such as Professor George P. Landow at Brown University, say that hypertext has the ability to revolutionize scholarship, analysis, and education.

Predicting the impact of technology is difficult at best. Not too long ago it was thought that microfilm would be the technology that would free researchers from the tyranny of the printed page. It didn't happen then, and I don't see evidence that it's happening now. But at least the new on-line technology promises to make the traditional library searches go faster. How thorough these cyber-searches turn out to be will critically depend upon the quality of the software that can perform these links.

Vehicles for the Highway

The stock market and its various connections to business and investors are a kind of "information highway," and few would deny that it is a very efficient highway. As information about a particular stock becomes widely known, the value of that information goes down. In the parlance of the market, it is discounted.

It's reasonable to assume that the same principle will apply to the Internet. Devaluation of information will occur as that information becomes more widely spread. This will result in a more level playing field with consequences that could be either positive or negative depending on the nature of the information.

In his book[42] Peter Lynch, the successful Magellan Fund manager, describes the stocks that he avoids. These are the stocks that every investor hears about in the car pool or on the commuter train, the stocks that everybody is talking about and few really understand. Curiously enough, these stocks often turn out to be among the high-tech stocks. As a prime example of this phenomenon Lynch features the Home Shopping Network, Inc. This information highway-type marketing company turned out to be a dog.

Recent government funding has been directed toward the effort to digitize materials in university libraries[18] so they can be accessible to computer networks. NSF, The National Aeronautics and Space Administration, and ARPA will award the money to six universities over the next four years. The project will pioneer new methods of collecting, storing, organizing, and retrieving information on networks. These grants are the federal government's largest commitment yet to aiding the construction of the "virtual libraries," which are presumably the vehicles that will ride upon the information superhighway of the future.

As one might imagine, this project is pivotal. Real innovations and breakthroughs are needed in order to make electronically available vast stores of knowledge and data. The six universities receiving the grants are

(1) Carnegie Mellon University: $4.8 million to study ways to digitize science and mathematics stored in video archives,

(2) Stanford University $3.6 million to work with NASA's Ames Research Center on developing an "integrated" library that could be used for searching large pools of scientific data,

(3) University of California at Berkeley, $4 million, to work on a digital library of environmental information and study new methods for intelligent search and retrieval,

(4) University of California at Santa Barbara, $4 million to work on ways to provide easy access to large collections of maps and aerial photographs,

(5) University of Illinois, $4 million to work on a library of journals and magazines in the sciences and engineering,

(6) University of Michigan, $4 million to work with several private companies on a library of multimedia resources in earth and space sciences. In each case the primary institution will work on the effort with other universities and private companies.

COLD FUSION

The cold-fusion affair was the first international "scientific event" in which the net played a central role. A recent book by Gary Taubes[67] chronicled the events of that time.

The dominant factor in the first week of the unfolding drama of cold fusion research was the lack of information. Martin Fleischmann estimated that in that time he provided details of his experiment over the telephone to several hundred scientists. Yet the information was not specific and did not contain sufficient detail to allow reproduction of the results. After the telephone and fax machines, the various computer mini-networks, fragmented precursors of the Internet, were the major source of information.

These networks had begun carrying requests for cold fusion information within hours of the March 23 announcement. It was, as writer and physician Lewis Thomas described it, a 'collective derangement of minds in total disorder,' played out on the infant cyberspace.

The net spread a combination of information, rumors, requests, and reports. Stan Pons had a computer and was connected through the network to the outside world; his electronic mail address had been disseminated on the net as well. Leaping ahead of any sobering and concrete experimental evidence, the net became a hothouse of café-styled theories to explain cold fusion.

The recent response of the Internet to the announcement of Robert McNamara's *mea culpa* book, "In Retrospect: The Tragedy and Lessons of Vietnam" was typical of the venom that often flows on the net. These viciously hostile e-letters are known on the net as "flames." The usual "threads," linked chains of messages, developed around the subject by many Vietnam vets and non-vets alike. Some called for a firing squad for the former Secretary of Defense, comparing him to Jane Fonda. Wrote one vet "...it is my fervent hope and prayer that one day McNamara's name evokes the same images and ideas as Benedict Arnold's does today."

CHAPTER 17

VIRTUAL REALITY-VIRTUAL NONSENSE

THE MYTH OF INTERACTIVITY

Look at you, last Saturday morning you sat for hours "surfing the Web," pausing to stop by in one of the "chat rooms," then on to look up the airline schedule for flights to Boston. Or, perhaps you downloaded one of the new Mortal Combat games and traded karate chops with the evil Khan.

Or did you instead go to the library to attend a lecture on works by the Chilean poet Pablo Neruda? Or perhaps you just sat outside the lecture room and thumbed through a few back issues of Popular Mechanics.

Perhaps the reality of last Saturday was that you had to mow the lawn and take the car down to the neighborhood service station to have the oil changed.

Which of these world experiences was the most interactive: the Saturday morning log-on, the trip to the library, or the weekend of chores that needed doing? And for that matter, what does "interactivity" mean anyway?

The term is a recurring mainstay of the computer revolutionary jargon. There is Sony Interactive, HarperCollins Interactive, Fox Interactive, Disney Interactive, and on and on. If you go to your local software store and buy a box of the stuff, chances are it says "interactive" on the outside. If it's not interactive, it's probably just a screen-saver. Interactivity is a foundation pillar of the PC culture.

Interactivity implies a two-way communication channel, although one of the participants is a machine. The user does not stand alone; perish the thought! This is another reason computer usage and mathematical thinking are at such odds. The mathematician thinks alone, or perhaps with another mathematician, but decidedly not interactively.

The initial experiences with computers were so humdrum and isolating that some device was needed to make them palatable to the masses. Interactivity was the answer. It was an answer that was particularly attractive to the advocates of traditional AI, since it implied that a thinking entity, the computer, was "interacting" with a human counterpart. AI has not succeeded in achieving such a thinking entity.

At best, interactive software creates an illusion of engagement with an airline-ticketing agent or with the evil Khan in a game of Mortal Combat. Interactivity as applied to software is a device to blur reality. In fact it can create multiple levels of reality ending with the ultimate in interactivity: virtual reality.

It's undoubtedly true that most good software is interactive. You input keystrokes, and then you are prompted to input more keystrokes, and finally something pops out: a graphical display, a list of numbers, a typed letter, etc.

The problem with interactivity is that is has been placed on a high pedestal and used to benchmark both computer and real-world experiences alike. The computer revolutionaries would have us believe that the more interactive the software is, the better it is. Thus came about the push to "multimedia," so that all of our senses could interact with the computer.

Virtual reality lies at the heart of the computer revolution, because it represents the ultimate blurring of reality, the ultimate in interactivity. Almost everything computers do imitates reality: simulations, modeling of physical processes, internet “rap rooms,” and even the familiar icons in the ubiquitous Microsoft Windows software are stand-ins for physical realities.

Some years ago at the University of Michigan's freshman orientation we were treated to a practice lecture by one of the professors. I suppose the purpose was to get us into the lecture listening mode and to jog our thinking. The lecturer told the story of a patient who visited a scientist, who wired him to a machine that could send visual, audio, and tactile signals to the patient's body. In fact the machine could send signals that could make the patient believe that he left the scientist's office and went on a trip, or went home, or went to a movie, or whatever.

The story had an unhappy ending with the patient going mad. After many trips to the scientist's office, he suddenly realized that he could never again know whether his life was real or virtual. The professor telling the story could not have guessed that less than forty years later, we would be presented with precisely the dilemma of the patient gone mad.

Minus the jargon, the practice of virtual reality has been around for more than twenty years. Aircraft simulation modules have trained pilots and measured proficiency in flying skills since the early seventies. The same idea is now being applied to a number of other tasks requiring manual dexterity and three-dimensional perception. Physicians can practice certain procedures in virtual reality such as gallbladder operations, engineers can design chips in 3-D[80], and astronauts can practice maneuvers in space without ever leaving the earth.

Another facet of virtual reality, probably the one that has made it so trendy, is its use in entertainment. Computer games have always had the aspect of virtual reality, but now they and the virtual reality thrill rides have taken on a new dimension, literally.

Plans are set for a giant, space-age virtual reality theme park right in the heart of London's buzzing Piccadilly Circus tourist and theater zone. Japanese video games giant Sega will help transform a major section of the park into a "Segaworld" theme park-the first outside Japan.

In a report to the May 1995 Congress devoted to the relationship between technological advance and human emotions Angelo Peluso, a Catholic sexologist criticizes the booming trend of "virtual sex." "The spread of virtuality in the sexual domain is becoming a worrying phenomenon," said Peluso. The Catholic Church is worried about the effect such fantasy can have on human behavior. "People are showing a tendency today to reject intimacy," Peluso said. "In this respect, the spread of cyber-sex represents an easy escape from the incapacity for responsible interaction between people. ... We must stop it before it is too late."

Other recent applications of virtual reality to aid geometric visualization may have more merit. CAVE (Cave Automatic Virtual Environment) is a prototype for a virtual-reality system at the University of Illinois[57] that lets scientists feel as though they have actually climbed inside what appear to be physical objects. A computer has created the "objects" from data supplied by the researchers. Among other things, the CAVE has been used to walk through geometric shapes, study molecules, and watch galactic events from a grandstand seat.

The first virtual reality systems required a user to don a heavy and cumbersome helmet that lowered a tiny television screen in front of each eye. As the wearer's head moves, the image changes to match an image that would be seen in the real world (i.e., reality). At the CAVE, the cumbersome helmets are replaced by high-tech eyeglasses only a little more substantial than sunglasses.

The computer that powers the CAVE currently has a list price of about $800,000. Some fancier systems allow for electronically wired gloves to be worn. One can then "touch objects" in the field of view with the glove, presumably disturbing them in some manner.

A few months ago the Doonesbury cartoon strip did a bit on such a set-up used by one of the principal characters to go on a "virtual shopping-spree." Indeed, one can easily imagine a cornucopia of "virtual world encounters."

The CAVE concept is somewhat different from earlier virtual reality concepts. Projectors behind the walls and ceiling create images on three walls and the floor in order to transform the room into anything the programmers have created. This accounts for the main virtue of CAVE in allowing for more than a single participant to enter the virtual environment. The perspective of the CAVE, however, is always centered on the operator with the location sensors; hence, the view of others is slightly distorted.

Some academics have been impressed by the power of the new technology. It has been used, for example, to simulate a walk along the fibers of chromosomes.

The value of CAVE, developed at the Electronic Visualization Laboratory at the University of Illinois at Chicago, is that scientists can benefit from 3-D images of molecules by discovering facets that are not accessible on a 2-D screen. In this case it is the molecule acetylcholinesterase, and the scientist is Richard E. Gillian of Cornell University. It turns out that this molecule is like a tiny machine, a vacuum cleaner as it were, complete with a little flap to pass other material. Apparently these 3-D aspects cannot, or at least would be very difficult, to visualize on a planar screen.

Electrical engineers soon will be forced to use virtual reality to design future generations of integrated circuits. The two-dimensional computer aided design (CAD) software has been around for quite a while, but future designs will require three dimensions.

In the past, engineers have designed integrated circuitry by relying on vertical, two-dimensional simulations of individual transistors and the other elements that make up typical microelectronic devices. But as these elements have shrunk in size, the interactions between the electrons and the edge of devices have become increasingly important. Consequently a third dimension is required to accurately model the circuit.

The new virtual reality software requires major gigaFLOPS (thousand million floating point operations per second) of computational power. As Robert Dutton, professor of electrical engineering at Stanford's Center for Integrated Systems, said, "...doing three-dimensional simulations of integrated circuitry is far more complicated than any of the computer graphics created for Hollywood."

VIRTUAL WORLDS

Virtual Museums

Carl E. Loeffler[3], a research fellow at Carnegie Mellon University's Studio for Creative Inquiry, with the help of an Egyptologist is trying to make it possible to "visit" the Temple of Horus, complete with Egyptian cats, to view animated hieroglyphics along the walls, and to approach a sculpture of Horus that will tell the viewer a little about that Egyptian who lived long ago. All you need to do this is to turn on your computer, don a "virtual reality" helmet, and enter cyberspace. Mr. Loeffler does not believe that virtual art museums will ever replace traditional ones. "...You take away our cathedrals, and you take away our museums, then what do you have as containers of the human spirit?"

Mr. Loeffler is looking beyond his virtual museum to a virtual city that he is designing-complete with apartments, stores, and a football stadium. What kind of people will a virtual city attract? "This will be particularly attractive for a category of person who spends a lot of time on these nets, who is more comfortable sending these smiley faces and interacting with people that way, than in this life as we know it," Mr. Loeffler says. WOW! This says worlds about the true import of virtual reality.

What might make more sense are the real-life museums that are on-line to some extent, i.e., on the Internet[17]. To mention a few: The Andy Warhol Museum (Pittsburgh), The Exploratorium (San Francisco), the Frederick R. Weisman Art Museum, University of Minnesota, the Michael C. Carlos Museum, Emory University, the Museum of Paleontology, University of California, Berkeley, the National Museum of Natural History, Smithsonian Institution, The Natural History Museum (London), the Peabody Museum of Natural History, Yale University, The Louvre (Paris).

Some museums feature audio-visual tours of their collections and allow viewing of text and images of exhibits, others allow electronic patrons to interact with various artifacts, such as rare musical instruments. The "Micro Gallery" program underway at the National Gallery of Art will allow visitors to gain in-depth information about more than 2,500 pieces in the gallery's permanent collection.

Recently, interesting applications of virtual reality have been made to the treatment of common phobias, such as fear of heights[63]. Psychologists have conducted clinical trials of patients with acrophobia. The patients were given 50-minute sessions of virtual reality treks across a plank extending toward a bridge without railings. Mountains appear in the distance, water below. Following the therapy sessions, many patients were able to complete real-word assignments of walking across a bridge or riding up and down 15 floors in a glass elevator while looking outside.

Other applications have been proposed. For example, psychologists in Japan are examining the idea of using virtual reality to calm cancer patients about to undergo traumatic chemotherapy.

What then is the future of interactive virtual reality? It certainly may have a future in the entertainment business and in all manner of training, but what we humans really want is to interact with other humans and our real world, not with a machine, however life-like the experience might appear. If we ever lose that desire, we probably will have lost our humanity.

CHAPTER 18

ARMAGEDDON: THE YEAR 2000

Charlotte, North Carolina, is the home of some of the largest banks in the nation. Except for New York City, it's the biggest banking center in the USA. Not surprisingly, it's also a big computer city. "Charlotte's home page @WWW.Charlotte.Com, better known as Charlotte's Web, extols the virtues of this Southern City of Commerce.

Bob Gruder, president of Alydaar Software Corporation based in Charlotte, was recently interviewed on the "John Boy and Billy" WRFX radio talk show. Bob explained to the radio audience the Year 2000 Problem and how it would affect almost everyone, not just in North Carolina, but all over the world.

Alydaar is in the business of "software reengineering." This just means rejuvenating and fixing old software that has been running on large mainframe computers for twenty or more years. Some of this software needs to be reengineered to run on more modern machines. A great deal of it has, what might seem at first blush, a trivial flaw.

For years most programmers writing software for the big mainframes (big iron) kept track of dates using two digits for the day of the month, two digits for the month of the year, and two digits for the year itself. This is fine for the days and months, since there are at most 31 of the first and exactly 12 of the latter. But what about the years? What's wrong with writing "97" for "1997?" We do this all of the time. On the face of it this shouldn't cause any trouble, because, when the century rolls over, you'll just write "00" on your checks. It may look a bit odd to see "01/01/00" at the top of correspondence going out on January 1 of the year 2000, but who cares?

Trouble comes in because software often computes with the two-digit year. For example, my auto insurance rates depend in part on the model year of my car (which happens to be 92). My agent runs software to calculate how much he will charge me in insurance premiums. This software checks whether the model year of my car is less than the current year (which happens to be 97) and by how much. No problem; it is, and I get to pay a lower rate since my car is five years old. What happens when he runs the same program in the year 2000? The software program is stupid; it will ask the same question: "Is 92 less than 00 (which is just 0 in the computer)?" "No!" The computer will answer. In fact, it will think that I'm a traveler from the future (2092) and god knows what it will charge me for insurance. This is the so-called "Year 2000 Problem."

What makes the Year 2000 problem a big deal is that flaws (bugs) of the above sort are replicated thousands of times over in the billions of lines of code running on the machines of virtually every large and intermediate sized company in the world: every bank, insurance company, airline, manufacturing and chemical company, and brokerage house.

Oh, yes, and don't forget to count the federal government. Social security, Medicare, and a host of federal programs make computations based on these two digit dates. Were you born in 1935? If so, you might be eligible for social security in the year 2000. Unless it is fixed, the software is likely to subtract 35 from 00 (or just 0 in the computer) to get a negative number! The stupid computer will think you are minus 35 years old, or what I suppose is the same thing, that you haven't been born yet! I guarantee that this will prevent you from getting a social security check.

All of these thousands and thousands of bugs will magically pop out when the hands of the clock (the clock inside the computer) move past 12 on that quickly approaching night of December 31, 1999. Still, there is something about the problem that rings trivial to fix.

Why not just change all the two digit dates to four digit dates? That's much more easily said than done.

Software is delicate stuff; changes of that type are incredibly laborious. It's not like using a word processor when you have misspelled a certain word throughout a document and can set matters straight in a moment by correcting its many occurrences with the stroke of a key. Nor can the computer clocks be turned backward or forward in such a way to alleviate or to at least postpone the problem. A computer needs to know the exact time and date that you and I agree upon and keep our appointments by.

It would even seem that the Pope could make a Papal Proclamation that will set the matter straight once and for all. Back in 1582 Pope Gregory XIII (after whom we have named our Gregorian calendar) straightened out the sticky business with leap years when there got to be a problem with festival and holy dates falling noticeably out of season. Let's just have Pope John Paul do it again!

No, this bullet is actually headed straight for us, and short of crash programs to fix the software in time, there is no way to avoid it. Many companies are rushing to fix their software in time. But a lot of time and money is required. By some estimates about $600 billion worldwide.

The Social Security Administration has been working for eight years since 1989 to change over their software so that it is "Year 2000 compliant." They say that they are only half done. At that rate they will have completed the changeover in the year 2005, or about five years too late. That's five years operating with a system that would be broken, one that could calculate negative ages for its recipients and spew out fountains of mangled data. If he were to get one, who knows what a recipient's benefit check might look like. Some would be for negative amounts. I guess that would mean that the recipient would owe the Social Security Administration money. Other checks would be for fabulous amounts, beyond the recipient's wildest dreams. It would certainly be a lot easier to fix the problem before it occurs.

What makes the problem even more insidious is that companies are reluctant to spend resources on a task that has no visible return. The software will not perform better or run more quickly after it is made Year 2000 Compliant. It's just that it won't break as a consequence of the century rolling over to 2000. Typically, a large brokerage house or insurance company will need to spend several million dollars to make its software compliant. That's a lot of money to spend with nothing immediate or visible to show for it.

Along comes Alydaar Software Corporation to the rescue! Alydaar will remediate your software for you, for a fee of course. As I have said, it's not that easy, so it might be worthwhile to explain the two basic techniques employed in the Year 2000 "fix."

The first approach, the straightforward one, that everyone, and you too probably, thought of right off the bat, was to simply expand all two digit year dates such as "97" so that it becomes "1997." What could be simpler? As it turns out, a lot could be simpler. First of all, how do I know that when I see the date "97" that "1997" is intended? There are instances, particularly when one is dealing with mortgages and insurance, that require encoding of year dates far into the future. It's not likely, you say, that "2097" was intended. After all, we'll all be dead and gone by that year. But what if the number were "30?" If it's a birth date, it's likely to be "1930," but if it's the maturity year of a long-term bond, it's more likely to be "2030." Additional code must be written so that the computer can tell the difference.

Another serious problem that arises with date-digit expansion is that two additional digits must inserted into the code. This eats up four additional "bytes" of storage space. On a given line of code, that may just not be available. In fact the expansion approach becomes so unwieldy and expensive to implement that Alydaar and similar companies have just about given up on this approach.

Most computer programmers in the past have coded the year using just two digits, i.e. neglecting to use the "19," since it was always assumed. The problem is that when the year 2000 arrives, the computers will assume it's 1900! All sorts of crazy things will happen.

You may get past due bills with an extra 100 years of interest-penalty added on, or you might get lucky and receive an extra 100 years of interest on your bank deposits.

It turns out that the quickest and cheapest fix for these old computer programs with the year 2000 flaw is not to go in and change all the 19s to 20s. In the first place, there are not many 19s in there anyway. It easiest to teach the computer how to do "clock arithmetic." You probably did some of this in the fourth or fifth grade. For example, you know that if you add 9 on the clock to 4 you don't get 13, because there is no 13 on the clock; instead you get 1 o'clock. Likewise, if you subtract 1 from 1 you don't get 0, because there is no 0 on the clock; instead you get 12 o'clock.

The clock arithmetic approach turns out to be cheaper than anything else, and that's largely the reason that it's most commonly used. The process begins by agreeing upon a 100-year interval, called the "window" or perhaps the "clock," that may be set to begin at any arbitrary two-year date such as 50. We then conceptually think of the window beginning with the year 1950 and ending with the year 2049. With this agreement the ambiguity of two year dates goes away. For example, if I specify "97," it's understood that I mean "1997," since "1997 falls within the window. If I specify "35," it's understood that I mean "2035," for the same reason.

How difficult then is it to implement the windowing approach to fixing old code having the two digit years? It turns out to be a lot easier than the expansion technique. The only thing that must be supplied in the code is the logic to correct for comparisons and operations with the old two digit years. We do this sort of thing all the time with the clock. For example, we know that one o'clock is later than 9'oclock on the same day if we know that the first time is PM and the second is AM. We make this adjustment even though the number "9" is larger than the number "1."

Likewise, in the case of the 100 year window we would say that 35 is later (further into the future) than 60, since by our agreement 35 falls in the 21st century. What's going on with the windowing process is just clock arithmetic and clock logic where the "clock" has 100 years on it instead of 12 hours.

It's been noted in the Information Science trade journals that whatever the technique for fixing the Year 2000 Problem, it's not "rocket science." Nor was it "rocket science" that caused the problem in the first place. Were programmers a mere ten to twenty years ago so shortsighted as not to realize the implications of their choice of two digits to represent years? These are ticking time bombs that the software managers allowed to be put in place. Did they believe that they would be out of the picture when the bombs exploded, or did they simply believe that the software, often written in one of the older programming languages, would be replaced before the bombs inside them would go off?

Not all of the consequences associated with the Year 2000 problem are humorous. I don't mean to imply that it's humorous to fail to get your social security check. There are, however, some consequences that could have disastrous and dangerous consequences. A lot of "firmware" will also turn bad unless it is replaced by the year 2000. This is software that is permanently embedded in every thing from toasters to military missiles.

Elevators in all of the big buildings of the country run on computer programs that monitor such things as last time to maintenance. They're programmed to shut down if that time is greater than some amount. What will happen on January 1, 2000? Using just the last two digits of the new year, 00, their computers may calculate that the last time they were serviced was about 98 years ago!

Harbingers of the impending apocalypse are already popping up. Computers at the Marks and Spencer food suppliers in Britain have ordered the destruction of tons of corned beef. The reason? They calculated the food's age at over 100 years. Visa has had to recall some credit cards with expiration dates after the year 2000. The computers calculated that they had already expired in the McKinley administration. A 104 year-old Kansas woman was notified to report to kindergarten in September.

According to Gruder of Alydaar Software, Swiss Air has plans to ground its aircraft December 31, 1999 rather than risk what might happen with software that regulates air traffic control. I know a lot of people, many of them at Alydaar, who also will refuse to be flying around the turn of the century.

Does the Year 2000 Problem represent a real impending apocalypse? Nah! We'll muddle through. But it sure does bring the machines down from their lofty pedestals and put things in perspective. We humans are still in charge.

CHAPTER 19

PC OR TV?

The personal computer and television technologies are beginning to merge and give birth to a single device. Both the PC and TV have always shared the identical principal interface, namely, the screen, or more properly, the CRT (cathode ray tube). But now as the major function of the PC to be the means of accessing the Internet emerges, the question has been rightly raised: Why have all of that on-board computing power? Why not just built a device that can upload and download data from the Internet? Sure, maybe you will need to keep the storage capacity, but there is almost no need to compute. Indeed, as applied to the PC, the very word "computer" has become a misnomer.

The latest in PC technology is precisely such a device, the Internet PC. It is minimal in the sense of being designed for the sole purpose of connecting to the Internet. In fact, you can use your old TV as part of the hardware.

Up until the present time the big difference between computers and TVs is that the former are digital, whereas the latter are analog. Basically, this just means that the signal processed and displayed by the TV is a continuous but varying electrical voltage. On the other hand, the data inside the computer have a digital, i.e. discrete, representation. With the advent of high definition TV (HDTV), however, even this distinction between computers and TVs will disappear. The HDTV will be a digital machine just like the computer. This technology is available today, but it will probably be a few more years before you will have to go out and buy a new TV. All of the hardware, both broadcasting and receiving, must be replaced with digital technology.

The TV-set industry will eventually cease to exist[45]. There will be a single device, still called the PC for personal communicator. It will be a TV, stereo CD player, computer, telephone; everything all rolled up inside a single box. Indeed, all of this technology is available now, and it's beginning to come to the marketplace. With an inexpensive microphone and card-insert for your PC you can talk long-distance with a family member in Casablanca, Morocco.

If further evidence is needed of the new trend, notice that almost all new PCs come equipped with a sound card and stereophonic speakers. If you don't want them, you have to make a special request to have them removed. Music can be played independently of other software in use. I enjoy listening to a Sibelius violin concerto (or the YMCA song) on my PC as I write this chapter!

This metamorphosis has already redefined the PC. There may still be a chip inside the box that allows it to make computations, but the word computer is becoming less and less applicable. It's not a computer; it's an electronic doorway to entertainment and to the Internet.

CHAPTER 20

BATTLES WON

Can the PCs in our schools already bought and paid for be put to good use? Yes indeed, they can display graphics in colorful and sometimes animated ways. Computer graphics can stimulate geometric intuition. A physical geometric model or picture is frozen in time, but computer graphics can show the evolution in time of changing geometry. In addition, computer graphics can use color to highlight the active parts.

The very best attempts to produce educational software are to be found among tutorials of geometry. Some of this software has been developed under the auspices of federal foundations, but many of the commercial packages provide some very entertaining as well as educational material.

Since before the time of computers, geometers have been a breed of mathematician who have long found value in and enjoyed the building of paper and wood models of geometric shapes. In recent times physical chemists and biologists have also found it useful to build models of complex molecules and lattice structures. A wood and paper model of a buckey ball has greater hold on intuition than does a verbal or analytical description of this newly discovered form of the element carbon.

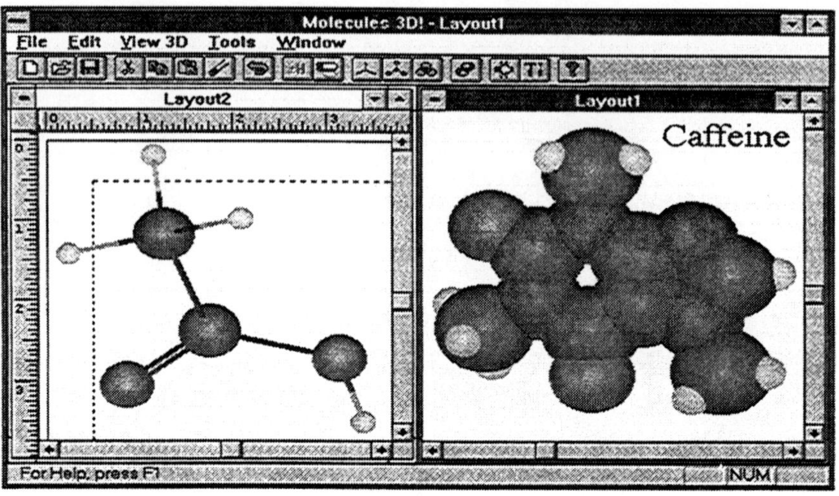

In place of the wood and paper models, computer graphics can be an alternative aid to the geometric intuition of students from kindergarten through college.

Computer graphics is not just for education. The very popular and successful animated movie "Toy Story" was the first movie to be generated entirely by computer graphics. Undoubtedly this is just the first of a genre that will add another dimension to movie making and to the use of computers for entertainment.

Thanks to computer graphics we can look out of the spacecraft window as we circumnavigate the moon or even Mars where no astronaut has yet gone. The computer is able to "stitch-together" hundreds of images taken from unmanned satellites that have gone before or sometimes simply from radar returns based on the earth. The result is a topographically accurate picture of what would be seen in an actual circumnavigation. What a wonderful capability the computer has to blur reality itself!

The era of digital photography is upon us. Bits (ones and zeros) will replace chemicals and the darkroom. This would have already happened except that the manufacturing cost of a high quality digital camera is still prohibitively high. The other components of digital photography are already commercially available at reasonable cost: software for your PC to process the digital photos and printers capable of rendering high quality pictures. Professionals who have dealt with this technology say that the digital rendering of shadows and certain colors is of higher quality than can be achieved by traditional chemical photography.

SOFTWARE: THE RIGHT STUFF

The best examples of software are to be found among the applications software or tools. There are excellent word processing packages, spreadsheets, and tools to generate attractive presentations of every kind under the shining sun. The user still has to provide the ideas and syntax, but easy to use software and a laser printer can lighten the clerical burden and make the final product look good.

There is excellent software to perform advanced engineering design and manufacturing, the so-called CAD/CAM (computer-aided design and computer aided manufacturing) software. Much of this has been quietly and effectively performing in the workplace for several years. It has not had much of an impact except on professionals, but for them the impact has been profound. Engineering designs that once took an engineer working closely with a draftsman weeks to complete now can be accomplished in days or less.

Even so, using this software, one is not likely to discover a new theory or even make a breakthrough in technology. But one could receive a lot of reinforcement to knowledge already gained, or even, perhaps, produce real work useful in daily applications of the workplace or of the marketplace. The CAD/CAM software will not think for the engineer. If one did not already have a firm grasp of the mathematics and physics behind this software, using it could be a very dangerous exercise indeed--something like an ape at the controls of a 747. Furthermore, simply running the software could not in a thousand years teach those fundamentals on which it is based.

My personal favorites of examples of the right kind of software are the products marketed by Wolfram Research, Inc. As a mathematician, I confess to a certain amount of prejudice in this selection. But frankly, it doesn't get any better than *Mathematica* by Wolfram Research, Inc. *Mathematica* is a software package, a higher order programming language if you will, which contains every built in function under the sun together with the routines to graph them in 3-dimensions of spectacular color and shading.

Although *Mathematica* is a very high-level language in the sense of being closer to English than most computer languages such as BASIC or FORTRAN, it is nonetheless intended for the fairly sophisticated user. One finds all of the common functions of engineering and school mathematics as well as examples having mainly theoretical interest to mathematicians such as the Riemann Zeta function.

One cannot use *Mathematica* to do research any more than one can practice the piano by listening to recordings of Chopin. But, nevertheless, it is enjoyable to do so, and, who knows, it may even be inspiring.

In addition Wolfram markets a line of add-ons to Mathematica, each in a special area. Thus, there is the *Finance Pack* and *OPERA* (Options, Pricing Environment for Research and Analysis), which enable the user to calculate a plethora of parameters related to stocks, bonds, options and other securities. Then there is *Optica*, a package allowing the user to carry out a vast array of calculations and make geometric drawings related to the functioning of lenses, lasers, illumination systems, mirrors, prisms, etc. All in all a delightful tool, one in which hours could be spent examining and reexamining all of the classical foundations of optics.

SUPER COMPUTERS

A super computer is an aggregation of smaller computers wired together with specialized software capable of performing many millions of operations per second. It works on the principle of parallel computing, which just means that a problem is broken down into parts, and the parts are simultaneously worked on. These computers are very expensive and generally only operated by large research scientific organizations. One company has held the lion's share of the super computer market, namely, Cray Research.

What good are the super computers? The answer is a lot! The output from these computers is able to simulate a multitude of complex interactive physical systems. The most familiar application is the modeling of global weather. Start with tropical depression Dolly in the Caribbean, key in some initial conditions such as local temperature and wind direction; mix carefully with a few meteorological principles, and Presto! The super computer can keep track of changes at each point of a fine grid that covers all of the possible tracks of Dolly. Your TV meteorologist can show a likely path of Dolly, whether she will get stronger, when and where she is likely to strike the coast. All of this magic is possible thanks to a super computer.

Super computers perform other useful tasks that enable engineers to test designs without having to actually build a physical model. For example, airflow over a newly designed airplane wing can be "tested" numerically by a super computer. Again, thanks to the computer's ability to make many simultaneous computations at each point of a fine grid covering the wing, the engineer can learn how the wing would perform if it were really built and tested in a real wind tunnel. Super computers are expensive, but not nearly as expensive as actually building and testing an airplane or whatever it might be.

COMPUTERS OF THE FUTURE

The future of computers is not the interactive type of PC that is now so popular. The word computer now conjures up an image of a PC sitting on someone's desk or perhaps of a large mainframe with tape drives spinning. In fact, both the form and roles of future computers will become highly fragmented and specialized. The word computer will become a generic term referring to many apparently completely different instruments.

Computers already have such unlikely forms as a pill to be swallowed by soldiers so that body temperature can be remotely monitored while the soldier is in the field. Although still expensive, there are computers to run every aspect of keeping you comfortable and secure in your house. These computers can monitor and adjust the ambient temperature, humidity, and lighting. They can monitor incoming telephone calls, warn of intruders, admit the delivery boy, and of course start coffee in the morning.

Computers will become more like unseen servants. And, except for some unusual circumstances, one does not ordinarily interact with a servant. A good servant serves quietly, unseen, like the chips in your car that "talk" with the chips in the toll booth and allow you to whiz through the toll-gate without your having to stop and fumble for quarters.

This past year a new company headed by the former CEO of AT&T opened its headquarters in Alexandria, Virginia. Its focus is on new technology that will allow wireless networking of computers. Imagine to be able to get onto the Internet without having to use a telephone line! When this technology becomes reality, the term “wired” will become instantly obsolete. Not surprisingly, the first issues that confront management have to do with frequency band allocation. The amount of available frequency spectrum is limited.

The data storage capacity and speed of computers has dramatically increased over a few years’ time. Back in the early 1950s, the dinosaur age of computers, the UNIVAC offered about 1,500 bytes of memory and was priceless. In 1983 a 20-megabyte hard disk (capable of storing 20 million bytes of information) cost $1,200.00; in 1995 a 1.3-gigabyte hard disk (capable of storing 1.3 billion bytes of information) cost $400.00. That is a 65-fold increase of storage capacity for a third of the cost! Moreover, the speed with which the data are accessed is vastly greater.

In thirty more years, the trend of these numbers will quite likely continue. In the year 2025 it should be possible to obtain high-speed access to hundreds of gigabytes of data at nominal cost.

This tremendous storage capacity will be needed by other technology presently under development. Examples of this are the voice recognition and synthesis systems. This technology is in its commercial infancy and much of it will have matured in thirty years. Computers, which are now controlled only by keyboard inputs, will accept voice commands and inputs. Computers, which now only send their outputs to a video screen or to a connected printer, will be able to aurally present their outputs as well.

Computers of 2025 will not be thinking any more than they do now, but it will seem so. If we attribute human qualities to computers today, we will do so even more when input-output (IO) is enhanced through the spoken word. Surely then computers will finally be endowed with human-like intelligence? I have serious doubts.

The mathematician Allan Turing conceived of his famous "Turing Machine," a machine capable of reading and writing 0's and 1's on an endless tape. This machine became the model for the development of modern computers and also a model for the AI theorist's concept of how the human mind functions at some primitive level.

The failure of AI to achieve its goal of building machines that have human-like intelligent behavior is probably due to our inadequate knowledge of the fundamental processes at work in the human brain. Some, such as Roger Penrose, believe that any attempt to create AI based on Turing's model is doomed to failure.

In fact, very recent research has shown that computers that have the capacity to adapt their outputs to data using, for example, the "neural net" technology are indeed more powerful than the simple machine that Turing envisioned. The definition of "more powerful" can be made precise. This research tends to support the thesis that traditional AI is on the wrong track.

Penrose[24] believes that there are processes at work in the human brain based on physics that is not yet known. He conjectures that quantum processes may be at work in the human brain, and therefore no computer based on procedural principles could ever achieve human intelligence. Until more is understood about the mechanisms of human intelligence, AI will not advance beyond the artifact stage.

PERSONAL COMPUTERS OF THE FUTURE

By the year 2025 the Personal Universal Communicator (PUC) will replace the Personal Computer (PC) of today. The PUC will perform all the functions of today's networked PC, fax machine, and telephone combined in a single unit. It will be your office away from the office, have memory capacity about a hundred times that of present PCs, and will maintain synchronization with your main office systems.

As far as hardware is concerned, it is by no means clear that the computer as we know it today based on semi-conductor, high-density integrated circuit design will be the computer of the future. Last November, Leonard Adleman of the University of Southern California astounded the computing world by creating the first "DNA computer."

Using the rules by which DNA's components bind to each other to imitate rules of logic, he was able to solve a "traveling salesman" type problem. Lately, Princeton computer scientist Richard J. Lipton has devised a DNA computation system that might be used to compute more difficult traveling salesman problems with logical side-conditions.

The traveling salesman problem is an important combinatorial problem having no known general algorithmic solution, so special cases of it provide a way of testing the capability of a computer of whatever kind. To put it another way, this is a problem that permits the benchmarking of computational power. So...perhaps the brain of tomorrow's computer will not be a silicon chip after all, but will more resemble a flask!

SOFTWARE OF THE FUTURE

Computer hardware capabilities have far outstripped the capabilities of the software to run them. Just the other day I heard of a new computer being installed that has one thousand megabytes of volatile memory. That's a thousand million bytes (computer guys like to say a "gigabyte") of memory for running software! I don't know of any computer programs that need that much memory, but the machines are waiting for them when they are written.

Software is a growth industry for the future. It hasn't done so poorly in the past ten years either. The US economy expanded by about 30% during the decade 1984-1994. The software industry expanded by about 269% during the same period to become the sixth largest manufacturing industry in the US.[40]

Advances in software will be just as spectacular as the advances in hardware. We have already made reference to the software that will enable voice recognition and synthesis (computers that talk). The future will also hold new and different kinds of applications software.

The AI spin-off that has born fruit is the so-called expert system. These are large computer programs that contain the facts together with many of the rules of inference pertaining to a specialized body of knowledge. The programs *Prospector* and *Mycin,* now over 20 years old, were among the first of their kind.

Prospector contained knowledge pertaining to geology and the discovery of valuable oil and mineral deposits. The program user would interactively input data and facts about a particular geographical region and respond to queries of the program. The computer would then, based on its rules of inference, output an estimate of what deposits one might expect to find there. At least one big discovery more than justified and paid for the development of *Prospector*.

Mycin and its descendant programs perform a similar function for the diagnosis of human diseases and ailments. Of course, a real doctor must always check and agree with the program's output before treatments to the patient can begin. Nevertheless, the time is coming when the reliance upon the outputs from such programs will be greater and greater.

By the year 2025 you will no longer have to struggle to do your taxes. Expert system software, which really already exists now, will do almost all of the work for you. Tax lawyers, and other lawyers as well, will have massive amounts of data at their fingertips and expert system programs to aid them in decision making.

Software "agents" of all kinds will monitor and make recommendations for the management of large corporations[40]. The people manager of today will become a manager of software tomorrow. The corporation's employees will be managed and directed by the "agents."

In fact, computers do teach and we do learn from them in the sense that any technology forces us to learn its principles and applications. Automobiles have forced us to master mechanics, heavier-than-air flight has taught us aeronautics, and computers are now teaching us programming, software design and hardware architecture. Computer technology stands in a unique category. As a technology it is very close to the human psyche. Because of this, there is a temptation to carry the anthropomorphic view of computers too far. In eliminating drudgery, they certainly may free up time, enabling one to spend that time on self-improvement. One might then have the time to learn philosophy or mathematics, but not from a computer.

CHAPTER 21

CONCLUSIONS

More than any other human invention computers reflect us. That single fact makes their impact so up close and personal. Our involvement with computers will probably outlive our association with any other machine: automobiles, trains, or planes. The computer revolution is here to stay; it may evolve and change direction, but another will not overthrow it.

At the moment personal computers represent the vanguard of the revolution and its most prominent feature. But the revolution also includes the mainframes, super computers, as well as the hundreds of guises that unseen computers have taken. The long and diverse list extends from the navigational computers on airplanes to the computers that control the environments and securities of buildings. All of these branches have blossomed just in the last three decades of the twentieth century.

The very word *computer* no longer reflects the most common use of the machine. A better term would be *communicator*. This is particularly true of the avalanche of commercial applications that are presumably transforming society. The usual applications call for no numerical calculations, or only very trivial ones. PCs are the principle vehicles for this new development. They are advertised as "multimedia" and have stereo sound, high-speed modems and of-course are networked. These machines are for communication, not computation.

As tools for computation the PC and calculator have been misunderstood in some quarters. The view that they correct for mental shortcomings, such as the inability to perform arithmetic operations, the way eyeglasses correct for imperfect vision is misguided and has dangerous implications. Computers do not "free" those who have failed to master the basic skills and thereby allow them to bypass these skills.

Calculators and PCs must find their appropriate place in the constellation of educational resources. They are for use ***after*** the underlying principles have been understood. Then, they can save valuable time when that time would be used in carrying out repetitive and routine calculations. They cannot be a shortcut to understanding or learning.

As tools for teaching children in the classroom, PCs have largely been failures. Test scores have not been raised, and there is other evidence that computers are not capable of teaching skills other than computer skills themselves. These skills are no substitute for the traditional basic skills of reading, writing, and arithmetic. To make matters worse, the marketing of computers throughout the nation has drained away valuable resources at a time when they could not be spared.

One of the principal reasons that computers and calculators can't teach is that almost by definition, they can't teach intuition. It is the innumerate, the numerical equivalent of the illiterate, who are the first to whip out their calculators when presented with a numerical problem. This is not to say that computers and calculators do not have a place, but this place is not a substitute for thinking.

The premise recently held by educators was that the more interactive software is, the better it is as an educational tool. Even highly interactive software does not encourage the student to develop independent ideas and thoughts. An increasing number of educators and computer makers are recognizing this fact. As a fix, they speak of machines that will become "bicycles for the mind." By some magic the PC will free the student to focus all his creative and artistic energies. This is at best a strained attempt to rescue the computer from oblivion as a tool for learning and at worst is pure marketing hype.

Proponents for the use of computers in the classroom can point to some isolated successes, particularly in the inner city schools where children do not otherwise have access to computers. But even these successes come about only indirectly. The kids didn't learn from the computers, but they were attracted by them and therefore were given a reason to attend school.

The failure of programs to develop computers that teach has paralleled the failure of programs to develop cognitive artificial intelligence (AI). No computer has been built that has the understanding or capability of a three-year-old child. AI has downsized and refocused its goals. Intelligent "artifacts" are the modern targets of this community. Software to imitate the behavior of an intelligent agent is one of the new goals. For example, an intelligent agent would look over a manager's shoulder, keep track of tasks accomplished and warn of tasks likely to fall behind schedule. Think of such an agent as an all knowing personal butler.

Computers, even the PCs, have excelled extremely well at computing, but almost nobody except for scientists and engineers uses them for that. The order of the day is the applications software that performs word processing, spreadsheet functions, bookkeeping, etc. This is all well and good, but it's not enough on which to build a revolution.

The success of the modern PC rests almost entirely on its ability to communicate with the outside world: e-mail, web surfing, and file transfers. Each of these functions, however, has an established competitor: the telephone, television, the fax machine, books sold at bookstores and checked out at libraries, and the US mail to carry ordinary letters.

Can the PC perform these tasks more cheaply? More quickly? You still need about $1,500 to $2,000 to get into the PC game. Then, once you've made his initial investment and paid your monthly subscription fee to one of the on-line services, you can begin to save money on e-mail over, say the telephone, or equivalently, the fax machine. Still, to recoup your investment and begin saving big bucks, you're going to have to write a lot of e-letters.

The issue of speed, getting information quickly, probably is the best reason to go with a PC. If you're lucky, you may be able to download the document you're looking for more quickly than you could get a copy from your local bookstore or library. And perhaps you will be able to peruse the artifacts in the Louvre on your PC long before you would ever have the time or money to fly to Paris and see the real thing.

The cliché that "The more things change the more they stay the same" applies in spades to the Internet. Only twenty-five years ago the future of cable TV was predicted to be like that of the Internet. Educational benefits galore would follow the "wiring-up" of institutions and private individuals.

Like cable TV, the Internet has been oversold as a highway to education. Its popularity is more reminiscent of the citizen-band radio fad of the recent past. Almost everyone I talk with says that he or she is on the Internet to get e-mail. Everyone is afraid of being left out. A few people speak glowingly of certain net functions, such as the capability to access airline schedules and make reservations on-line, just like travel agents have done for more than twenty years. But all of this just doesn't add up to a revolution. Much is promised, and much money has already been made and spent. If the single promise of being able to easily access the contents of libraries and museums of the world comes to pass, the Internet will at least have fulfilled one important revolutionary promise.

Beyond the issues of utility and productivity, the PC satisfies a basic human urge to tinker. Instead of going out to the garage on Saturday morning to work on the old jalopy, Joe Homeowner goes to his den and "logs on." Now with the World Wide Web and various other browsers for the Internet the PC can become a virtual time-sink: a place of escape from having to paint the bedroom or fix that leaky faucet in the downstairs bathroom.

I don't know of any statistics on the subject, but among my personal acquaintances I believe that the "tinker factor" provides a major impetus for the PCs popularity. Even before the Internet there was much to do to keep busy at the PC. I know at least two people who have several PCs at home. These individuals set up a local area network (LAN) for themselves, although I can't imagine why one would want to do that at home. Clearly the tinker factor was at work. Come to think of it, that's how the computer revolution got started in the first place: William Shockley and John Bardeen tinkering around in one of Bell Telephone's labs and inventing the transistor back in 1948.

REFERENCES

[1] Achenbach, Joel, "Wire Me Up, Scotty," Washington Post Magazine, May 29, 1994, page 11.

[2] Baer, Walter S., "Cable Television: A Summary Overview for Local Decision Making." National Science Foundation Research Applied to National Needs Program, 1973 (February), 134-NSF, Santa Monica: Rand

[3] Bard, Steven, "Carnegie Mellon Researcher Invites You on a Trip to 'Virtual Reality'", Chronicle of Higher Education, September 14, 1994.

[4] Barry, John A., *Technobabble*, MIT Press, Cambridge, Mass. 1992, page 207, page 208

[5] Bork, Alfred, *Learning with Computers*, Digital Press 1981

[6] Boston, Nigel and Andrew Granville, The American Mathematical Monthly, May 1995, page 470

[7] Bowen, William, "The Puny Payoff from Office Automation." Fortune, 26 May 1986

[8] ____, *Personal Computers for Education*, Harper & Row, New York, NY, 1985

[9] Brod, Craig, *Techno Stress*, Addison-Wesley, Reading, Massachusetts, 1984

[10] Brynjolfsson, Eric, "The Productivity Paradox of Information Technology," Communications of the ACM, December 1993.

[11] Buoy, Roger, VNU Business Publications Inc., Personal Computing, October 1988, p 290

[12] Conley, William, Chronicle of Higher Education, October 6, 1995, page B4

[13] Crawford, Trish, The Toronto Star Newspaper, April 9, 1995

[14] Daly, Christopher B., "Simpson Murder Trial Teaches Real-Life Lessons to Harvard Law Students," Washington Post November 6, 1994

[15] DeLoughry, Thomas L., "EDUCOM Conference Focuses on Ways to Improve Teaching," Chronicle of Higher Education, November 9, 1994

[16] _________, "Gatekeeping on the Internet" p. A21 Chronicle of Higher Education November 23, 1994

[17] __________, "Museums Go High-Tech," Chronicle of Higher Education, September 14, 1994

[18] _________, "Government Provides $24-million for 'Virtual Libraries' Projects," Chronicle of Higher Education, October 5, 1994.

[19] __________, "For the Community of Scholars, 'Being Connected' Takes on a Whole New Meaning." Chronicle of Higher Education, November 2, 1994.

[20] __________, "'Fair Use' for Electronic age: Debate Over Copyright Law Heats Up," Chronicle of Higher Education, September 28, 1994.
[21] __________, "Mandatory Computers," Chronicle of Higher Education, May 5, 1995, A37.
[22] Dreyfus, Hubert L., *What Computers Still Can't Do*, MIT Press, Cambridge, Massachusetts, 1992
[23] Duncan, John, "The White Heat of Technology," in The American Mathematical Monthly, page 194, Volume 102, Number 3, March 1995
[24] Dunham, William, *The Mathematical Universe*, John Wiley & Sons, 1994
[25] Dvorak, John C., PC Magazine, The Computers-In-Education Fiasco, 10/08/96,
[26] Evans, Sandra, "Bookworms Go Electronic," Washington Post, May 22, 1995
[27] Forester, Tom & Perry Morrison, *Computer Ethics*, MIT Press, 1990, page 140.
[28] Freedman, David H., Brainmakers, Touchstone, New York, 1994
[29] Gates, Bill, *The Road Ahead*, Viking, New York, 1995
[30] Gebhardt-Seele, Peter G., *The Computer and the Child*, A Montessori Approach, Computer Science Press, Inc. Rockville, MD, 1985
[31] Gelerntner, David, *The Muse in the Machine*, The Free Press, New York, 1994
[32] Geraghty, Mary, "Pen-Based Computer Seen and Tool to Ease Burden of Note Taking," Chronicle of Higher Education, November 9, 1994.
[33] Gillen, Marilyn A., Billboard Publications, Inc., July 30, 1994
[34] Hadamard, Jacques, *The Psychology of Invention in the Mathematical Field*, Dover Publications, 1945
[35] Horgan, John, "The Death of Proof," Scientific American, October 1993
[36] Jacobson, Robert L. "Scholars Plan a 'Virtual University,' Offering Courses Exclusively on the Internet," Chronicle of Higher Education, November 16, 1994
[37] Kennelly, Jim, "Ways Going ON-LINE Can Change Your Life," Washington Post Magazine, September 1994
[38] Landauer, Thomas K., *The Trouble with Computers*, MIT Press, Cambridge, Mass, 1995
[39] Lacampagne, Carole B., "Transforming Ideas for Teaching and Learning Mathematics," Office of Research U.S. Department of Education, page 9, July 1993
[40] Leebaert, Derek, (Editor), *Future of Software*, 1995, MIT Press
[41] Leiby, Richard, "Future Schlock," Washington Post, December 4, 1994.
[42] Lynch, Peter, *One Up on Wallstreet*, Simon and Schuster, NY 1989
[43] Mills, Mike and Corcoran, Elizabeth, "Clinton Plan Would Wire All Schools." Washington Post, October 11, 1996, page A1
[44] Negroponte, Nicholas, "The Sunday Painters," The computer Age, M. Dertonsos and J. Moses (Eds.) Cambridge, The MIT Press 21-35.
[45] ____________, *Being Digital*, Vintage, New York, 1996
[46] Neumann, Peter G., *Computer-Related Risks*, ACM Press and Addison-Wesley Publishing Company
[47] Newquist H.P., *The Brain Makers*, SAMS Publishing, Indianapolis, Indiana 1994

[48] Papert, Seymour, *The Children's Machine*, BasicBooks, New York, 1993
[49] ________________, *Mindstorms Children, Computers, and Powerful Ideas*, Basic Books, New York, 1980
[50] Paulos, John, A., *Innumeracy*, Hill and Wang, New York, 1988
[51] Provenzo, Eugene F., Jr., *Video Kids: Making Sense of Nintendo*, Harvard University Press, Cambridge, Massachusetts, 1991.
[52] Ragosta, M., Holland P.W., and Jamison, D.T. "Computer-assisted Instruction and Compensatory Education: The ETS/LAUSD Study, Executive Summary and Policy Implications," Princeton, N.J.: Educational Testing Service.
[53] Roszak, Theodore, *The Cult of Information*, Pantheon Books, New York, 1986
[54] Vos Savant, Marilyn, *The World's Most Famous Math Problem (The Proof of Fermat's Last Theorem and Other Mathematical Mysteries*, St. Martin's Press, New York, 1993.
[55] Schank, Roger C., Cleary, Chip, *Engines for Education*, Lawrence Erlbaum Associates, Hillsdale, NJ, 1995
[56] Schwartz, John, "School Gives Computer Sex the Boot," Washington Post 11/6/94.
[57] _________, "Flickering on the CAVE Walls, Reality in another Dimension," Washington Post, November 28, 1994
[58] Scully, John, *Odyssey*, Harper & Row, New York 1987, p 405, p 247
[59] Shear, Michael D., "Adding Up Pros and Cons of Calculator Craze," Washington Post, November 20, 1994
[60] Shen, Fern, "Mouse, Modem and Identity!" Washington Post, April 25, 1995, page A1
[61] Siegel, Lenny and John Markoff, *The High Cost of High Tech*, Harper & Row, New York 1985
[62] Solomon, Cynthia, *Computer Environments for Children*, The MIT Press, 1986
[63] Stevens, Jane E. "Flights Into Virtual Reality Treating Real-World Disorders," Washington Post Science Section, March 27, 1995, p A3.
[64] Stoler Peter, *The Computer Generation*, Facts on File Publications, New York, NY, 1984
[65] Stoll, Clifford, *Silicon Snake Oil*, Doubleday, New York, 1995
[66] Suplee, Curt, "Discovery 'Simplifies' 4-Dimensional Equations," Washington Post, December 6, 1994
[67] Taubes, Gary, *Bad Science: The Short Life and Weird Times of Cold Fusion*, Random House 1993.
[68] Thomas, Susan Gregory, Software that Turns Kids On, US News and World Report, December 2, 1996
[69] Van der Knapp, Coenrasd, "The Educational Software Market in the Netherlands," American Consulate - Amsterdam, Feb. 1993
[70] Wall Street Journal, November 30, 1984
[71] Wilson, David L., "A Year after Reorganization, EDUCOM Plans to Announce A Series of High-Profile Projects," Chronicle of Higher Education, November 2, 1994

[72] ______, "A Key for Entering Virtual Worlds," Chronicle of Higher Education, November 16, 1994
[73] ______, "The Appeal of Hypertext," Chronicle of Higher Education, September 28, 1994
[74] ______, "A Death en Route to the Data Highway," Chronicle of Higher Education, October 5, 1994
[75] Wilson, Kenneth, and Bennett Davis, *Redesigning Education*, Henry Holt & Company, New York, 1994
[76][a] May 22, 1996, Rene Sanchez
[b] June 19, 1996
[c] June 14, 1996, Rene Sanchez, page A1
[d] June 16, 1995, Amy E. Schwartz
[e] December 6, 1994, Curt Suplee
[f] June 22, 1996, "NJ School's High-Tech Myth"
[g] June 14, 1995, Rene Sanchez, page A1
[h] June 19, 1995, page A1
[I] May 22, 1996, Rene Sanchez, page A1
[77] Unger, J. Marshall, *The Fifth Generation Fallacy*, Oxford University Press, New York, 1987
[78] ABC News Report, May 8, 1997, Peter Jennings
[79] DATAMATION, May 15, 1990, page 92
[80] Edge Publishing, Work-Group Computing Report, March 27, 1995
[81] General Accounting Office, Newsbytes News Network, April 10, 1995
[82] Japan Computer Industry Scan, Kyodo News International, Inc., January 23, 1995
[83] Notices of the American Mathematical Society, Vol. 42, No. 7, July 1995
[84] US Bureau of Labor Statistics, 1995 Abstract
[85] U.S. News and World Report, Cover Story, December 2, 1996
[86] U.S. Government DOE Press Release, "Gore, Riley Present National Technology Plan to NET DAY Participants," July 2, 1996
[87] Reuters (USA), May 18, 1993
[88]Computerworld, June 8, 1992

INDEX

4

4GLs, 99

A

America, iv, vii
American Samoa, 69
America-on-Line, 123
Arkansas, 78
ARPA's (Advanced Research Projects Agency), 121, 131
artificial intelligence (AI), 2, 3, 9, 10, 11, 14, 31, 32, 33, 34, 40, 48, 55, 56, 69, 136, 159, 160, 161, 165
ATM services, 107
Australia, 28

B

BASIC, 54, 156
bulletin board systems (BBS), 122

C

calculators, 14, 17, 18, 19, 21, 22, 29, 39, 40, 42, 43, 80, 81, 82, 164
California, 71, 72, 73
carpal tunnel syndrome, 115
CAVE (Cave Automatic Virtual Environment), 138, 139, 171
China, 121
Citizenship, v
CompuServe, 123, 127, 129
computer aided design (CAD), 7, 139, 155
computer aided manufacturing (CAM), 7, 155
computer software, xiii
Coordination theory, 110
Copyright Act, 87
Cray Research, 157
CyberBanking, vii, 126

D

Defense Advanced Research Projects Agency (DARPA), 3

E

education, 72
EDUCOM, 66, 67, 169, 171
e-mail, 4, 24, 85, 86, 109, 113, 116, 122, 123, 124, 125, 126, 129, 165, 166
end-user, 100
Euclid, 91
Europe, Eastern, 113

F

fatigue, computer, 8
Fifth Generation Project, 11
flash cards, 23
FORTRAN, 25, 156
Four Color Theorem, 93
free speech, 84

G

Gauss, Carl Frederick, 91
gender stereotyping, 63
Global Learning and Observations to Benefit the Earth (GLOBE), 127
Greece, 86

H

Hadamard, Jacques, 49
Hawaii, 54, 69
health care, 128
high definition TV (HDTV), 151
House of Representatives, 127

I

India, 113
Information Superhighway, vii, 4, 119
information technology (IT), 100
Internet, 1, 4, 23, 44, 68, 71, 72, 84, 86, 87, 109, 118, 120, 121, 122, 123, 124, 125, 126, 127, 129, 130, 131, 132, 133, 151, 152, 158, 166, 169, 170

J

Japan, 11, 28, 137, 141

K

Kansas, 148
Kasparov, Garry, 39
Kentucky, 26, 75

L

local area network (LAN), 68, 167
Logo, 12, 35, 36, 52, 55, 56

M

Mao Zedong, 121
microchip, 106
minimum wage, 113
Minsky, Marvin, 2, 31
Missouri, 72
Montana, 15
Montessori methods, 56
Morocco, 152

N

Neanderthal, vi
New York, iv
New Zealand, 86
Nintendo, 61, 62, 64, 171

P

Papert, Seymour, 23, 31, 35, 52, 55
Pennsylvania, 84
Personal Digital Assistants (PDAs), 108
Personal Universal Communicator (PUC), 160

Q

quality of life, 17

R

Radiation, low-level electromagnetic, 115

S

Sagan, Carl, 79
social security, 144

T

telecommunications, 118, 127
Texas Instruments Inc., 20
thin client, 100
Tiananmen Square, 120
Turing, Alan, 9

U

UNIVAC, 158
UNIX, 100, 111

V

Vietnam, 133
violence, 63
virtual reality, xii, 6, 7, 44, 136, 137, 138, 139, 140, 141, 142
virtual surgery, 6

W

wide area network (WAN), 68
Wisconsin, 77
World Wide Web (WWW), 123

Y

Year 2000 Problem, xiii, 143, 144, 148, 149